"In Thirty minutes, you'll be hanging from a
ROPE
in front of the courthouse square!"

Audacity
Story of a Legendary Hero

Connie Williams

By
Connie Williams

The author of *Emily's Blues; Green, Jon and Lale's Dance; Confession of the Onion Ring King; This Life: Through Grace Hope and Mercy*

Audacity Story of a Legendary Hero

By Connie Williams

Audacity Story of a Legendary Hero by Connie Williams, are actual accounts of events and based on true history, interviews and research. Some parts presented October 2012 at the "Lynching Without Sanctuary" conference, the University of North Carolina, at Charlotte, Center City campus. Some parts included in an earlier publication: of *Green,* April 2018.

© Copyright 2019 by Connie Williams TX u 2-159-085 Text and compilation of photographs researched by Connie Williams. All rights reserved by the author. Including research, interviews, and news clippings gathered for the presentation and this publication. No part of this book or parts thereof may be reproduced in any form or copied without the prior permission in writing from the author/publisher. The scanning, uploading and distribution of this book via any other means without the permission of the author/publisher is illegal and punishable by law. Please do not participate in or encourage electronic piracy of copyrighted materials. Your support of the author's rights is appreciated. Correspond via Cmae77@att.net

Published by A Williams Acorn Publication *AWAP*

Cover Photo of Robert Franklin Williams. John H. Williams photos: University of Michigan, Bentley Library

Book design by Connie Williams

ISBN 978-0-578-96228-3

Printed in the United States of America

Audacity: Story of a Legendary Hero   Connie Williams

Contents

Introduction	5	The Conference: UNCC
Chapter 1.	14	Early Life of our Hero
Chapter 2.	18	Course of his Life
Chapter 3.	25	Someday I'm Going Back South
Chapter 4.	28	Education
Chapter 5.	31	Life-Changing Event NAACP
Chapter 6.	34	Desegregation of the Library
Chapter 7.	36	Don't Intend to be Lynched
Chapter 8.	44	The NRA
Chapter 9.	49	National Outrage: Kissing Case
Chapter 10.	54	KKK Vowed to Kill RFW
Chapter 11.	60	Epilogue of Green
Chapter 12.	63	Lawrence Kohlberg Analysis and Emily
Chapter 13.	75	Epilogue from GREEN
Chapter 14.	80	Lawrence Kohlberg and Robert Williams
Chapter 15.	86	Undermined faiths in Civil Law
Chapter 16.	92	KKK Intimidation
Chapter 17.	98	Williams-King-Malcolm
Chapter 18.	100	If Heinz were Black
Chapter 19.	102	I am a Man—Will walk Upright
Chapter 20.	106	Psychosocial "Turning Point"
Chapter 21.	110	Williams in Cuba
Chapter 22.	119	Williams in China
Chapter 23.	134	Return to America
Chapter 24.	142	Scapegoat Justice
Chapter 25.	147	Compilation
Chapter 26.	161	Commentaries
Acknowledgments	190	
Chronology	196	
Notes	199	
Bibliography	206	
Internet	213	
About the author	216	
Commentary	220	
Other Publications	225	
Blank	236-237	

Dedicated to all of the people

INTRODUCTION

Before the writing of this book Audacity Story of a Legendary Hero, a conference was held at the University of North Carolina, Charlotte Center City Campus. I communicated the following email to Dr. J. Leak, Director of the Center for the Study of the New South:
Greetings Jeffrey:

After careful review of the premise and ideologies of the featured presenters such as: M. Berg; F. Brundage; CC Clegg and A. Wood, I believe the civil rights struggle of my hero, Robert Franklin Williams, should add credit to the collective philosophy and practices against racism, lynching and attempts to oppress humans, especially Blacks, in an effort to systematically prevent them from participating in the free enterprise market, under Jim Crow.

I am happy to announce my intent to present my findings at the October Conference on "Lynching."

Re: Proposal consideration "Lynching in America" Conference

Date: May 31, 2012

Story of a Hero and Anti-Lynching

Quite a few states did in fact lynch more white people than black. In the West a greater number of white lynchings was due to political reasons not racial reasons. California, Colorado, Indiana, Iowa, Kansas, Michigan, Minnesota, Montana, Nebraska, New Mexico, North Dakota, Oklahoma, Oregon, Utah, Washington, and Wyoming lynched more whites than blacks (Chesnutt 206).

However, unlike the West, in the South, in places such as Monroe, North Carolina, black persons not yet tried in a kangaroo court could find themselves lynched by mobs of whites without justification. This is a story of anti-lynching and Robert Franklin Williams.

****

Leak, Jeffrey
To: Williams, Connie M
Friday, June 29, 2012 3:08 PM

You replied on 6/30/2012 10:26 AM.

Dear Connie:

Your abstract for the Without Sanctuary Conference has been accepted. We look forward to your presentation. Below you will find the link to our website that has much of the information you will need for the conference, but certainly contact me if you have any questions. Thank you for your intellectual work, and we hope to see you in October.

Best,
Jeffrey

Jeffrey B. Leak, Ph.D. | Associate Professor of English
Director, Center for the Study of the New South
UNC Charlotte | Department of English
9201 University City Blvd. | Charlotte, NC 28223
Phone:

****

Williams, Connie M
Actions
To:
Mr. Leak, Jeffrey

Cc:

Williams, Connie M.
Inbox, Sent Items, Top of Information Store
Saturday, June 30, 2012 10:26 AM

Hello Jeffrey,

This story introduces the episodic events of Robert Franklin Williams' modes of reasoning related to his difficult life and decisions making practices to avoid being destroyed (lynched) in a small town Monroe, North Carolina in America.

Thank you for this great news: that my submitted proposal abstract was presented, accepted and approved. I look forward to the conference and being in touch.

Ironically, I am attending our Robert Franklin Williams' (the hero of my proposal) family reunion this weekend. This will be exciting news to share with them.

Sincerely,
Connie Williams, M. Ed. | 1101/1102 Lecturer |
Writing and Inquiry in Academic Contexts I and II
UNC Charlotte | Department of English

To begin our hero's journey, I must first talk about the concept and practice of "lynching" that was always in the A). forefront of our hero's mind, and B). the concept and practice of lynching was also the focus of the conference held, and my own participation to address lynching related to our "hero" at the conference.

The "Lynching Without Sanctuary" Conference gathering was held in the month of October, 2012 to 1)represent and interpret the controversial stories, 2)images, 3)literary explorations of lynching 4)threats, struggles against racism, 5)oppression and denial of human rights, 6)the role of lynching in America culture, particularly associated to the South.

First of all, the conference commemorated some vital historical events of that same month, and it commemorated the removal of antiquated racists restrictions. One such occasion as that of Minister Dr. Martin Luther King Jr. the youngest recipient of the Nobel Peace Prize, awarded forty-eight years earlier, October 14, 1964; the legislators wanted to reward the renowned civil rights icon for his use of civil disobedience via nonviolence to try to end racial discrimination and Jim Crow.

Secondly and fortunately: Since this conference of October 12, 2012 was a 21st Century event in time, the obnoxious, offensive Jim Crow had been stripped of his power among the intellectual members of this discourse community who congregated to tell the stories of common and uncommon cultural, social experiences, insights and histories void of human restrictions predicated on the pigmentation of one's skin: and restraints such as having to enter the back doors to be seated in back of the room which was customary during segregation.

The following content, in part, is an edition of the presentation I, Connie Williams, shared at the conference.

****

The Conference Speech

The purpose of this discourse I will reflect upon the violence, race ideology and Southern history during the 50s and 60s in Monroe, North Carolina, highlighting events that could have led to our hero Robert Franklin Williams' lynching. *Audacity: Story of a Legendary Hero*, this historical narrative of Robert Franklin Williams life is to reveal his astounding acts related to active defiance, self-reliance and civil rights. My plan is to elaborate on the chronological events of Robert Franklin Williams life; his lynch-mob escapes, and heroic acts which led to his hounded exile with his family by the FBI into Canada, Cuba and then China.

I will explore the idea of Quality of Life over Blind Obedience of the Law—Constructive Use of

Defiance and Civil Disobedience as they apply to Robert Franklin Williams' thinking and his effort to "stand up" for his oppressed people against Kangaroo Courts functioning under the influence of Jim Crow in the 50s and 60s.

I shall not attempt to tell these horrific life events through "rose-tinted glasses" nor paint acceptable visuals.

The Introduction to the conference presentation ends here.

****

Following the UNCC, Center City conference conclusion, in my later years, I have spent my time continuing this life story and research to advance the subject to new levels. I will use the term, "fivefold." This new level is fivefold whereas: I will [1]focus upon our hero Robert Franklin Williams' life and thinking; paralleled to [2]Emily's life, thinking and actions reflecting similarities to our hero's (RFW) thought processes from the book *Emily's Blues*. [3]Moreover, this discourse will be inclusive of the "Epilogue" from the book entitled *Green,* as it relates to the eleven year old protagonist's Emilee and RW's (main characters in the double plotted book), their simultaneous horrific experiences during the race riot in Monroe. [4] I want to apply

Lawrence Kohlberg's hypothesis, the psychologist who theorized about a wide range of issues related to moral development in both psychology and philosophy, [5] The focus will be inclusive of the psychosocial approach of Erik Erikson concerning cultural-based development and his theory of fidelity and self-esteem, measures of "Morality and Racial Identity Development" (Cross et al 1990); ...African American Child.... applied to Robert Franklin Williams' mode of moral thinking--a turning point from childhood to adulthood related to our hero (Harris et al 2007).

Briefly: Lawrence Kohlberg's Level III, Post conventional, autonomous, of principled, is considered the highest level of thinking. In revealing the story, I will endeavor to indicate in the case with Robert Franklin Williams, that there is a clear effort to define moral values and principles that have validity and application apart from the authority. Kohlberg's Level III has two stages: Stages 5 and Stage 6 of moral development, as I believe, and hopefully we shall see, they helped motivate our hero Robert Franklin Williams' mode of thinking and actions: his "audacity."

Additionally, and predominantly, I also want to demonstrate how this hero, Robert Franklin Williams, took the necessary actions of self-defense and defiance against unjust laws *because he wasn't willing to allow the Ku Klux Klan and "Scapegoat" Supremacist—lynch mobsters to make a community event with his precious life by hanging him in the courthouse square as the police chief of Monroe promised!*

Furthermore, our hero, Robert Franklin Williams wasn't willing to add to the southern atrocities by allowing the lynching mobsters to make a community viewed spectacle with his body—his "God-given temple" like the lynched black bodies that continue to appear on display in photographs and documentaries at museums such as the Levine Museum of the New South and numerous museums perhaps around the world such as the National Memorial for Peace and Justice in Montgomery, Alabama; where steel columns dangling from beams with names carved into the steel symbolizing lynched victims; and where at the Legacy Museum also in Alabama, jars displayed in exhibit with soil from the site where a Black man was set on fire, hanged and dragged. Williams once said "I wasn't going to allow the white man to have that kind of control over me."

Chapter 1. Early Life of our Hero

When the mastermind stepped in front of the Monroe, NC judge at the old Union County courthouse building, he had out witted the scapegoat supremist racists so called "grand wizard", and the chief of police Mauney's plot to hang him from a tree in front of that very same Union County court house square. He had escaped the 500 sleigh dogs into exile whose motto was "We always get our man." He escaped the 2K angry mob threating to pour gasoline on him and his followers, some included Richard Crowder, a local nineteen-year old youth, elected chairman of the Monroe Non-Violent Action Committee and seventeen year old Harold Reep from Monroe. He had escaped the FBI's Most Wanted Armed and Dangerous Dragnet for a pretentious kidnapping charge. He had become the president of the NAACP. On or about September 4, 1969, Williams purchased a ticket for air passage from Dar es Salaam to London, England via United Arab Airlines, and thereafter from London by direct flight to Detroit, Michigan on Trans World Airlines. And now he stood before this judge. Him with rugged mixed-gray beard, dark eyeglasses, militarily cladded and Army military hat. He felt he could wait out in Detroit while the erroneous kidnap charge was being dropped. Then as soon as his plane touched down on Michigan soil, the authorities immediately arrested him for extradition to North Carolina for the phony kidnapping charge.

Little had been known, when this man was an infant born to Emma Carter Williams and John Lemuel Williams, that he would progress to become known in England, Germany, Italy, France, Rome, Belgium, Spain, Africa, Vienna; Rotterdam, Vietnam, Cuba and China for the humanitarian good deeds accomplished. He placed his life on the line for his fellow man. And these good deeds should be learned and talked about, studied and remembered in the many parts of the world of his remarkable life story making its mark in history as an extraordinary, legendary hero.

The hero, Robert F. Williams was born on February 26, 1925 in a two story house on Boyte Street, in "Newtown." He had two sisters, Lorraine Garlington and Jessie Link; and three brothers, C. Howard, John H. Williams and Edward S. Williams. Robert was next to the youngest child. My cousin, the hero came up during a corrupt law enforcement hierarchy and irresponsible political system-- whites only—Jim Crow Law era.

Robert Franklin Williams' grandfather, Sikes Williams and my father Jones McConnie Williams' father Reverend Daniel Arthur Williams my grandfather, were brothers. Sikes Williams (Robert's uncle) was one of the first college trained school teachers in Union County. He attended Biddle University which became Johnson C. Smith University. Sikes taught his wife Eller Tomlin Williams who also became a teacher. Robert Franklin Williams' uncle was the principal of a school. Williams' grandmother was a former slave. His grandfather, a Republican, who supported President Lincoln, the Republican who wrote and signed the Emancipation Proclamation, owned a printing press and published a local newspaper called *The People's Voice* (Burns).

Williams grew up with his siblings in a seven-room, two-story home on Boyte Street in Monroe. The house no longer stands in the historic district of Monroe. Once the home was torn down, another older house was moved onto the lot--a subtle way of erasing African American history and a part of our hero's past.

Robert Franklin Williams could have followed the course for his life as a railroad worker like his father John Lemuel, or like his Uncle Sykes, he could have become a school teacher. But as fate would have it, the course of his life was chosen for him when he vowed as a youth to be different—to take the path paved with civil disobedience, and the dangerous road to overcome systemic racism. He chose the difficult and dangerous path and became a Civil Rights leader. As a railroad worker for Southern Railroads: Seaboard Coast Line that became a branch of the Southern Railway in 1940s. The Georgia, Carolina & Northern Railroad started at Monroe, NC in 1887 and was built to Atlanta. Robert's father and many Blacks held important jobs with the railroad whose responsibility among others was to turn the trains around at the roundhouse before they left the station. Through the railroad jobs, many blacks earned more money than most Negros of the area. In spite of the unemployment under Franklin D. Roosevelt and the Great Depression, the families' work afforded them a huge two-story home in a part of the black ghettos. This area did not always contain dilapidated houses and deteriorating projects, nor were all of its residents poverty-stricken. The ghetto was "home", a place representing authentic blackness and a feeling, enjoyment, or emotions, a by-product of rising above the strife and anguish of being black.

Chapter 2 The Course of his Life

Robert Franklin Williams attended Winchester Avenue School in Monroe, the city's only African-American school for many years. There at Winchester he took an interest in history, geography, and writing. Though his school books portrayed slavery as socially beneficial, he nevertheless was stirred by the brutal aspects of racism at an early age.

It is believed that ethnicity (family background) influences our perception of who we are, and how we react to danger, privileges, depravity, disrespect, and violence perpetrated upon us and other humans. Robert Franklin Williams knew his validity distinctive of his parents and extended family deriving from his primary discourse community—home, family, language; and secondary discourse apprenticeship—community, church, and school experiences (Swales 1990).

At an early age Robert's mother Emma Williams read to her children; Robert Williams was raised on stories from the Bible and tales from his former-slave grandmother Ellen about his grandfather Sikes, who stumped North Carolina for the Republican Party during Reconstruction; who was a part of the biracial Populist-Republican alliance (Republicans and Populists in state executive offices, and a non-Democratic state supreme court. A significant number of cooperationist officeholders were African American. Fusion produced the only departure from Democratic Party hegemony after Reconstruction) and published the before mentioned newspaper in the 1900s called The People's Voice, (A paper for dealing with the black people and against certain kinds of oppression). The paper adhered to a radical democratic vision whose authors asserted that if "the enlightened Southerners (black Republicans who allied themselves with white working people who had organized on the basis of economic interest against the business-oriented "Bourbons" of the Democratic Party) declare themselves in favor of free schools and a free ballot, simple justice and equal opportunities for all men, we will meet them halfway, whether they were abolitionists or slaveholders" (Fusion Party 1800s).

According to Tim Tyson, "Born in the hopes and agonies of Reconstruction, persisted African American communities, black Southerners developed an expansive vision of democracy in their effort to secure the fruits of emancipation. Into such a community Robert Franklin Williams was born, and he became an heir to this outlook." *Radio Free Dixie*: (1999).

Ellen taught her children and grandchildren values. This was exemplified when before she died, Ellen Williams gave young Robert the rifle which his grandfather had wielded against white terrorists at the turn of the century. The rifle was one of the family's prize possessions which also became a representation of family pride to Robert, her young grandson.

Young Robert's initial experience with violence and white supremacy during his childhood are causes for civil disobedience, which are expounded upon in this narrative; yet, they certainly influenced his vision of self-protection and direct action taken to defend innocent, downtrodden, demoralized and attacked persons. Williams unfortunately came face to face with racism early in his life. Even as a youth, he made a conscious decision to defy unjust law. As early as the age of eleven in 1936, Robert Franklin Williams practiced civil disobedience (civil disobedience is a public, non-violent and conscientious breach of law undertaken with the aim of bringing about a change in laws or government policies), even before he was mature enough to fully understand the practice and its meaning.

We envision fate's compelling hand in Williams direct action against unjust law, when consequently, a devastating experience that continued to play upon his psyche of a dragged, defenseless black woman bloody and beaten with clenched fist by a white man in his attempt to take her off to jail.

This experience was so unequivocally devastating that it caused this very young person (a child) to move into action—he prearranged a surreptitious group with friends called the X35 to make combat on supremacist seducers who "openly practiced"—in front of the divine and everyone, a systemic double standard—humiliation and violence against the black woman in daylight, but who sought black women after dark. Reminiscent of images of the brutality leveled upon the dragged black woman still in his memory, when an unambiguous car drove through a shadowy, isolated section of Newtown in search of black women for lusty contacts, Williams along with the cooperation of his friends, let loose an unexpected avalanche of bricks and stones, smashing the car windows, sending the bigoted charlatan screeching off. Williams used defiance at this early age to protect black citizens from the exploitation of whites. A clear example of a hero's sense of right and wrong and civil disobedience.(all humans' right for decency should be protected not violated)—those laws are valid insofar as they are grounded in justice, and that a commitment to justice carries with it an obligation to disobey unjust laws—a law that did not protect humans on the basis of the color of their skin.

Thereafter, these actions placed the young eleven year old Robert on an inevitable path for becoming a target for hanging in Monroe as early as the 50s.

Similarly, as Williams enters his teens at age sixteen, he soon recognizes a frightful reality that legislation and the courts orders tend only to declare rights they can never thoroughly deliver—the rights handed down to all citizens in the Declaration of Independence and the Bill of Rights: The right to Life, Liberty and the Pursuit of Happiness—these are ideals that the American citizens and their government would fight for.

At age 17 in 1942, Williams became discouraged on the home-front with what he witnessed as weak legislature. He ultimately left high school to receive vocational training as a machinist with the National Youth Administration (NYA). After his education at NYA camp near Rocky Mount, North Carolina, he continued his studies at Elizabeth City State Teachers College (now Elizabeth City State University), an all-black, teacher's college in Elizabeth City, North Carolina.

During World War II, again, young Robert was faced with deliberate racial discrimination causing him one year later to take a segregated bus to Detroit to work at the Ford Motor Company to gain employment in the city's thriving war industry. Living with his oldest brother, Edward, he worked at Ford Motors. After 18 months of profitable employment in Detroit, Williams faced the destructiveness of racial tensions again—the outbreak of the 1943 race riot where he unfortunately experienced one of the worst race riots in US history. An experience most youths his age, his white counterparts, most would venture to say, would not have experienced or have any knowledge of and would ever encounter or suffer.

Several contributing factors of the riot revolved around **police brutality**, and the sudden influx of black migrants from the south into the city, lured by the promise of jobs in defense plants. The migrants faced an acute housing shortage which many thought it would be reduced by the construction of public housing. Consequently, young Robert Williams fought in the Detroit Riot of 1943, when he witnessed white mob killings of dozens of black citizens. The race riot took place from the evening of June 20 through the early morning of June 22. But, was ultimately suppressed by the use of 6,000 federal troops. It occurred in a period of dramatic population increase and social tensions associated with the military buildup of World War II, as Detroit's automotive industry was converted to the war effort. Existing social tensions and housing shortages were exacerbated by the arrival of nearly 400,000 migrants, both African-American and White Southerners, from the Southeastern United States between 1941 and 1943. The new migrants competed for space and jobs, and against white European immigrants and their descendants. Like the successive rebellion that would erupt 24 years later, the Detroit Race Riot of 1943 was deeply rooted in racism, poor living conditions and unequal access to goods and services. The apparent industrial prosperity that made Detroit the Arsenal of Democracy masked a deeper social unrest summer of 1943. The KKK was active in the region and the rioting.

Chapter 3 Someday I'm Going Back South

Some months later, following the Detroit Race Riot, Williams was involved in then another brief stint as an auto worker in Detroit.

In the days that followed, rioting spread across the city, resulting in 34 deaths. Shortly thereafter, Williams took a six-month job at the Mare Island Navy Yard near San Francisco. Unable to tolerate the outbreaks of racial violence that occurred in the employee dormitories there, he quit and returned home to Monroe. Back in Monroe, Williams earned his high school diploma and wrote poetry and prose-works that appeared in *Heartstrings Journal* and *Westminster Magazine*, as well as a weekly column in the *Monroe Enquirer*. His short story, "Some Day I Am Going Back South," was published in the *Daily Worker*.

During World War II, Williams was drafted into the Army in 1944, and served for 18 months, fighting for freedom in what Malcolm X would consider "a white slave-masters' segregated Army."

Williams was sent to Fort Bragg, North Carolina. After earning high scores on a radio aptitude test, he was transferred to a Signal Corps battalion at Camp Crowder, Missouri, to be trained as a radio operator. To his disappointment, however, he was assigned to a school for telephone linesmen. Before completing his telephone line training, he became ill and was re-assigned as a clerical typist.

In the months following World War II, Williams experienced the effects of low morale that spread among Camp Crowder's segregated black troops. Defiant of the harsh treatment by white officers, Williams was confined in the camp stockade for insubordination. Robert Carl Cohen writes in his book *Black Crusader*, "Williams was proud of being in the stockade because he felt he was there for resisting an unjust system-not for committing a crime" (2014). In 1946, after a six-month stay at Fort Lewis Washington, Williams received an honorable discharge.

Following his discharge from Camp Crowder, he returned to Monroe. Once back home in Monroe, in 1947 at the early age of twenty-five, Robert Williams became the husband to the youthful sixteen year old Mabel Ola Robinson; to this union his children: Robert F. and John Chalmers were born; both are now deceased. Arm and arm beside her husband, Mabel later fought for and carried out the rights of armed self-defense against the vicious attacks of the Ku Klux Klan, militantly representing the liberation struggle of her people, sharing her husband's commitment to social justice and African-American freedom.

Chapter 4 Education

Under the educational benefits of the G.I. Bill, which allowed members of U.S. armed forces to pay for their college education, Williams attended college and studied courses in psychology and creative writing at West Virginia State College. During his year there, he joined the staff of the college newspaper, *The Quill*. He consecutively transferred to North Carolina Central College in Durham, where he studied literary classics and read the works of Karl Marx and Vladimir Lenin introduced to him by a group of college communists. In the fall of 1950, he sequentially continued his study of literature at Johnson C. Smith College (now Johnson C. Smith University) at Charlotte.

When his G.I. benefits expired, Williams additionally was unemployed. In 1952 he went to New York City to look for employment. While living with an aunt in Harlem, he then became employed at the Curtis-Wright aircraft plant across the river in New Jersey. During this stay in New York, he befriended a group of white left-wing intellectuals, some of whom were active in the American Labor Party. (In 1936 the American Labor Party (ALP) was formed by left-wing supporters of Franklin D. Roosevelt and the New Deal). With the fall of war production, Williams lost his job at the aircraft plant and returned to Monroe again.

Desperate to support his family, he traveled to New York once again, and he found employment as a laborer on a farm in upstate. In the *Black Crusader*, Robert Cohen wrote, "Sharing the lot with migrant farm workers proved to Williams that exploitation isn't limited to the cotton fields of Dixie or to blacks" (1972).

Nearly destitute and only 29-years old, Williams raised bus fare and traveled to Los Angeles to work as a machinist in the city's aircraft plants. As it would happen, by the time of his arrival, however, the post-Korean War recession had left few employment opportunities. Unable to find a job, he joined the U.S. Marine Corps in 1954 to be trained as an information specialist. Instead of receiving training as a data specialist as he had been assigned, he underwent special combat training at Camp Pendleton, learning the use of rifles, machine guns, grenades, rocket launchers, and various infantry weapons. The battalion, nicknamed the *Magnificent Bastards*, is based out of Marine Corps Base Camp Pendleton, California and are a part of the 5th Marine Regiment and 1st Marine Division. Robert Williams was an outspoken opponent of racial segregation in the armed forces and refused to salute the flag at a celebration parade. Following his action, at the ceremony, Williams was sentenced to 180 days in the compartment of a ship where prisoners are confined, a place of detention—the brig. His candor concerned the Marines, who placed Williams under investigation. Upon his release, he underwent special mountain warfare training in Nevada. Prior to boarding for a tour of duty in Korea, Williams was discharged.

Chapter 5 Life Changing Event: the NAACP

When Robert Williams departed the Marine Corps, he knew he wanted to return home and he had ambitions to join the NAACP. Not long after his return to Monroe in October of 1955, Williams, joined the predominately white local Unitarian Fellowship and the Human Relations Group--a coalition of Unitarians, Catholics, and Protestants. Williams's increasing civil rights activity prompted him to make an important decision that would eventually change the path of his life: to join the Monroe NAACP as well. At the time of his return to Monroe, there was a small and dwindling chapter of the organization. The Union County NAACP was a typical Southern branch—small, not very active, dominated by and largely composed of, the upper crust of the black community—professionals, businessmen and white-collar workers. According to Williams in his book *Negroes With Guns*, "Before the Supreme Court desegregation decision of 1954, the NAACP was not a primary target of segregationists—racists were not too concerned with the small local chapters. Following the Supreme Court decision, this drastically altered the casual attitude. The Ku Klux Klan; the White Citizens Councils located any local chapter officers and members to threaten violence and apply economic sanctions to make people withdraw their membership." Chapters that were already small decreased swiftly.

In 1957, at age 32, Robert Franklin Williams became the president of the National Association for the Advancement of Colored People (NAACP) and civil rights activist, and at that time, he had a devoted and idealistic belief in the Constitutional rights and equal protection under the law for all people especially the oppressed. Williams announced in the *Monroe Enquirer*, "All citizens who believe in democracy, the rights of man, and brotherhood are urged to join and support the NAACP. This organization is open to all people, irrespective of race, who support the American cause as embodied in the United States Constitution."

With an endeavor to increase membership, he walked into the Negro poolroom in the town, interrupted a game by introducing the NAACP literature on the table and made a pitch which therefore he recruited half of those present. This began a drive among most Negro people in the area of Monroe, which changed the dynamics of the chapter because of the working class composition and the leadership that was not middle class. Williams writes, "most importantly, we had a strong representation of returned veterans who were very militant and who didn't scare easily." Also, he turned to Dr. Robert Perry, Woodrow Wilson, and John W. McDow, with whom he had stood against the Klan in 1947 in a confrontation in front of the Harris Funeral Home. These three devoted menfolk—fathers were independent entrepreneurs, upstanding citizens and family men who were fiercely loyal to Williams (Potter 2003).

As president of the Monroe NAACP in the late 1950s, Williams watched as members of his community were denied basic rights, tormented and brutalized by the KKK, and ignored in the courts. Seeing no other recourse, he began to advocate "armed self-reliance" (taking a militant stance against racism) to oppose what could have been another hundred years of beatings, bombings, aggressions—regular brutalization at the hands of whites. Up until then, black opposition meant only by the means of nothing except "soul strength" and holiness in the face of white terrorism. Members of his NAACP chapter, void of equal protection under the laws of the Constitution, began to engage in armed self-reliance to protect their families and homes against the Klan with rifles and sandbag fortifications.

Chapter 6 Desegregation of the Library

Following the 1954 U.S. Supreme Court decision Brown *v. Board of Education of Topeka*, which called for an end to the "separate but equal" doctrine, in 1957 Williams as active president of the NAACP sought to respond to the end of separate but equal practices. To apply the new doctrine at a timely period in history, he sought to desegregate Monroe's Union County Library. Though he expected an unforgiving battle, yet, with the support of a Unitarian group of white people the board chairman agreed, without complaint, to desegregate the library. After this incontestable first triumph, Williams proceeded to desegregate Monroe's municipal swimming pool. If Robert Williams preconceived any outlandish trouble and opposition to integrating the library, when it came to integrating a "whites only" Country Club swimming pool, he doubtfully hadn't determined the outcome predicated on his success for the library.

Outraged over the deaths of several black children in backwoods swimming holes, another horrific experience that helped shape Robert Franklin Williams decision making processes was his concern about unjust laws and systemic double standards.

The drowning death of a young black boy in a nearby lake in summer of 1957, aroused Williams' keen humane sense of right and wrong, and as a man he was led to campaign for safe swimming rights so that young black youths could enjoy the same safe swimming privilege as their white counterparts.

He refused to allow little black boys to lose their lives in mud holes, while the use of their tax dollars went to support a segregated public facility for white children who swam in the Monroe Country Club swimming pool. The Country Club "whites only" pool provided safety instruction and swimming lessons each summer, which by the way, alluded to earlier, were paid for with tax payers' dollars. He called upon the Freedom Riders who came to Monroe in bus loads to demonstrate and show support in an attempt to end segregation. A large number of Monroe's middle class and blue-collar blacks supported the campaign.

****

Chapter 7 Ideology for Nonviolence—Attempt to follow the law: International attention

Robert Williams believed in the laws of the Constitution and Martin Luther King's ideas of nonviolent protest. Williams's attempt to carry out this same ideology for nonviolence was shown through the thoughtful organizations to protest. It was recognized, King countered with an eloquent distillation of nonviolent philosophy but acknowledged that even Gandhi recognized the moral validity of self-defense.

When Monroe officials refused to integrate the swimming pool, Williams first gained international media attention in early 1958 with the swimming pool demonstration. Here again, this made Robert Franklin Williams a target for hanging. Whites wanted Williams and his followers to wait and accept a promise of building a separate pool for blacks at an unspecified future date. While demonstrating at the pool, which was inclusive of family members, Monroe citizens and Freedom Riders, Whites shot at Mr. Williams and the picketers with guns. Consequently, rather than allow Blacks' swimming privileges, the town filled in the pool with concrete to avoid it becoming integrated.

When the pool was closed, the racists decided to handle the matter in "traditional Southern style"—they turned to violence, unlawful violence. According to Robert Williams, "We had been picketing for two days when we started taking lunch breaks in a picnic area reserved for 'White People Only'. A group of white people started firing rifles and we could hear the bullets strike the trees over our heads. The chief of police was on duty at the pool and I appealed to him to stop the firing into the picnic area." (Williams 1958).

In response to Williams's request to stop the dangerous firing at the picketers, the chief of police said, "Oh, I don't hear anything. I don't hear anything at all."

"The following day the shooters drifted toward the picket line firing their pistols and we kept appealing to the chief of police to stop them. He would always say, "Well, I don't hear anything." (Williams 1958).

Mr. Williams' attempt to follow the law failed, and when he reported to the police chief the life-threating event toward him and his people being shot at during the swimming pool demonstration, responding sarcastically, Chief Mauney cynically uttered, "No, I didn't hear any gunshots."

Robert F. Williams replied, "It's good that you can't hear, because you won't hear it when we start shooting."

In the meanwhile, the Klan began rallying and numbers grew to 7,500 who gathered in fields to discuss how they would deal with what they called "Communist-Inspired-National-Association-for-the-Advancement-of-Colored-People." A push designed to drive Williams and Dr. Perry and the followers out of the community. *But when the Klan discovered they couldn't intimidate Williams, they proceeded to other "mob violence tactics—Scapegoat Psychology": forming KKK motorcades to parade through the community honking horns, firing pistols from car windows, victimizing innocent women in the streets.*

When a group of Negro ministers appealed to the Monroe city officials to prohibit the Klan motorcade from parading through the streets, the officials of the county and the city rejected the request on the premise that the Klan was a legal organization and therefore exercising their constitutional rights to organize the same as the NAACP.

"We sent a telegram to the U.S. Justice Department asking them to protect our right to picket. The Justice Department referred us to the local FBI. The FBI in Charlotte said this was a local matter that *they* had checked with our local chief of police, who had assured them that he would give us ample protection. This was the same chief of police who had stood idly by while those people were firing pistols and rifles over our heads" (Williams 2013).

On Sunday, on his way to the swimming pool, Robert Williams passed through U.S. 74 and U.S. 601, where today stands our grandfather's church: AME African Methodist Episcopal Church, where there were approximately two to three thousand white people lined along the highway. As Williams drove his car to the intersection, a car driven by a white man backed out as fast as it could, with an attempt to overturn Williams's vehicle and struck the front causing it to go into a ditch. The crowd started screaming "A nigger hit a white man. Kill the niggers! Kill the niggers!" The man who struck Williams's vehicle jumped out with a baseball bat and began walking toward Williams and the carload of picketers. He was saying, "Nigger, what did you hit me for?" Williams and the other occupants said nothing. They just sat in the car looking at him. When the aggressor with the bat came close and raised the bat, Mr. Williams put an Army .45 up in the window of the car and pointed it right into his face without saying a word.

Under North Carolina state law it is legal to carry firearms in your automobile so long as these firearms are not concealed. Consequently, the aggressor began backing away from the car. Someone in the crowd fired a pistol. Some of the crowd began throwing stones on top of Williams's car, they screamed, "Kill the nigger; pour gasoline on the nigger." Williams opened the door of his car, putting one foot on the ground and stood up in the door holding an Italian carbine. At this point three policemen had been standing about fifty feet away from Williams's car.

Williams and the picketers kept waiting for the policemen to come to their rescue. "When the mob saw we were armed and that they—the mob couldn't take us, the policemen began running. One policeman ran straight up to the car and demanded, Surrender your weapon! Surrender your weapon! I struck him in the face knocking him back away from the car and put the carbine in his face. I told him; we are not going to surrender to the mob." I told him **"WE DON'T INTEND TO BE LYNCHED!"** (Williams 2013).

Another policeman ran around the side of Williams's car started to draw his revolver out of the holster hoping to shoot Mr. Williams in the back. The policemen didn't know Williams and the picketers had more than one gun. One student, J. Covington, a seventeen year old, put a .45 in the policeman's face and told him, "If you pull out that pistol, I'll have to kill you." The policeman started backing away and put his gun back into the holster.

An old white man in the crowd started screaming and crying like a baby; kept crying and screaming and had to be led away.

The only way Robert Franklin Williams was saved that day was through the works of his Mighty Lord and his *audacity* to face mob violence with determination and self-reliance. He requested protection from the Monroe City Councilman among the crowd along with the police chief to open the highway to allow Williams's car to move away. Without some opposition, the man from the City Council led them through the mob. By the time Williams arrived at the pool, the other picketers had already begun the picket line. There were three or four thousand white people milling round the pool including city officials and the mayor. Again, the police chief came up and said, "Surrender your guns." Williams informed him, "I am not going to surrender any gun. These guns are legal and that is a mob out there, and if you want the guns you can come to my house and get them after I get away from here!"

Then the police chief AA Mauney said, "Well if you hurt any of these white people here, God damn it, I'm going to have to kill you!" Finally, the City Councilman appeared again and said "If you are willing to go home, I will see that you get escorted." The City Councilman suggested that the police chief escort Williams. But Williams told him, he might as well go with the KKK. City Councilman asked Williams what he suggested that they do? Robert Williams suggested they contact the state police, and soon an old corporal and a young man came; just two state patrolmen. The city had twenty-one policeman present who claimed they couldn't keep order.

The old corporal started cursing at the crowd to move back and move out of there while swinging his stick. They saw that he meant business and began to break up and disperse. Two police cars escorted Robert F. Williams and the picketers out—one in front and one behind. This was the first time the white people had witnessed something like this being done. And some of the white people started screaming "Look at how they are protecting the niggers! Look how they are taking niggers out of here."

As a result of Robert F. Williams' willingness to fight, to protect himself and the followers, the state of North Carolina had enforced law and order against mob violence: Providing a clear example that the Constitution applies to all people, with "equal protection under the law."

Williams anti-lynch movement against the mob ended that afternoon something the crowd preferred, an all too common occurrence, an afternoon lynching.

This obviously and clearly solidified Robert Franklin Williams once again as a target for hanging.

"For a black man to stand up for his equal rights in the early 1960s was unfathomed—impossible to comprehend…" In the words of Tim Tyson in his book *Radio Free Dixie*, "…but when a white man's rights are threatened, he will react with vehement force." (Tyson 1999).

Chapter 8 Robert Williams's Anti-Lynch Movement   (Shrewd Anti-Lynch Politics)

Effectively following the shooting at the swimming pool demonstration, Monroe's black community intent to undertake a program of armed self-defense established themselves within a year of obtaining a gun club charter from the National Rifle Association (NRA). The National Rifle Association of America is a gun rights advocacy group based in the United States. Founded in 1871, the group has informed its members about firearm-related legislation since 1934, and it has directly lobbied for and against firearms legislation since 1975.

Founded to advance rifle marksmanship, the modern NRA continues to teach firearm safety and competency.

Robert Franklin Williams recruited 60 members who armed themselves with military surplus weapons and mail-order firearms. As quoted in *White Violence Black Response*, Williams recalled how his self-defense unit "spent the summer in foxholes behind sandbags. We had steel helmets. We had gas masks. And we had a better communication system than they have now."

Consequently, death threats against Dr. Perry, the black doctor and vice president of the NAACP in Monroe caused Williams to post a 24-hour vigil outside the doctor's home. On October 5, 1959, while the Klan made a routinely night ride through Newtown, they unexpectedly met the fire of Williams's defense guard. In *Making of Black Revolutionaries*, writer James Forman described the scene: "It was just another good time for the Klan...." Near Dr. Perry's home their revelry was suddenly shattered by the sustained fire of scores of men who had been instructed by Williams not to kill anyone if it were not necessary. The firing was blistering, disciplined, and frightening. The motorcade, of about 80 Ku Klux Klan cars, which had begun in what the Klan considered a spirit of good fellowship, disintegrated into chaos, with panicky men stripped of their "good time" fleeing in every direction. Some abandoned their automobiles and had to continue on foot" (Forman 1972).

Robert F. Williams and Dr. Perry, Woodrow Wilson, John McDow and others were overwhelmed with death threat when Williams began to strap his .45 automatic pistol, which was legal, making clear his intentions-the necessity of what he called "armed-self-reliance." The Robert Williams's anti-lynch movement of the 60s. A movement began by Williams that demonstrated: We (me and my Black brothers and sisters) don't intend to be lynched! I term it: anti-lynch politics (a keen practical sense and acute mental discernment/soundness of judgment—shrewd. The use of intrigue or strategy in obtaining any position of power or control). Williams said, "As long as I was talking, merely talking, I had a lot of white liberal support, but when I actually started arming people and picking up guns, they said I had gone too far." The fight against racism and the consensus among well-meaning white and blacks began to break down.

Inasmuch as a consensus breakdown began to weaken the fight against racism, our hero, Robert Franklin Williams refused to allow the Supremacists mobs to ride through the black neighborhoods of Newtown in Monroe, terrorizing families, throwing bricks and bottles, shooting at houses and killing innocent black people. After organizing the Rifle Association, calling upon membership, like my father, the late Jones McConnie Williams, WWII Army Fifth Division veteran, and first cousin to Robert Franklin Williams, was called upon to service the artillery, clean, maintain the group's rifles and handguns.

I can intensely recall as a young girl of eleven, how terrified my mother, I and my siblings were when my father attended those clandestine meetings held at Dr. Perry's home. These are unforgettable scenes featuring many of the iconic events elaborated upon in the "Epilogue" of my book *Green, Story of A Hero (Robert F. Williams) and Anti-lynching* 2017. Both *Green* and *Audacity: Story of a Legendary Hero* tell the captivating stories of these two young persons, RW and Emilee learning about violence and a world dominated by hate before, during and after the maturation processes.

A former event in Williams' life; that lasting image had fostered his decision making process of self-reliance when the Ku Klux Klan (KKK) wanted to lynch the deceased body of a black man in 1946. Bennie Montgomery was a friend of Robert Williams, and a recent returning African American veteran, who had been executed by lethal injection for killing his white landlord during the disagreement over sharecropping. When the body was sent to Harris Funeral Home in Monroe, right there on Winchester Avenue, where Robert Williams attended school, astonishingly, the Klan felt they had been deprived of their hanging, warned "the body belonged not to the family, but to the "invisible empire."—"Scapegoat psychology."(Scapegoat theory is a social psychological term that relates to **prejudice**. According to this theory, people may be prejudice toward a group in order to vent their anger. Blame someone else for one's own problems).

Williams and his group of former soldiers, standing in front of Harris Funeral Home with forty rifles aimed at the Klan's line of cars stopped them from hanging Montgomery's deceased body. I reiterate (the body that had already been executed by lethal injection). Hereafter, this event convinced Robert F. Williams beyond a doubt, that black southerners had to be willing to jeopardize everything to confront white supremacy, deciding that self-defense was required and proven to be a more powerful strategy than civil disobedience!

Chapter 9 Kissing Case more National Outrage

Williams' keen sense of astute intellectual wisdom allowed him to "see through" a situation and decide whether that situation is good or bad. This action caused his life to be put on the line once again in October, 1958 when he refused to allow two little black boys ages eight and ten to lose their lives. The **Kissing Case** is an incident that sparked protests and legal challenges related to the Civil Rights Movement around the globe in England, Germany, Italy, Belgium and Spain.

The police and the mayor charged two black boys, seven-year-old David "Fuzzy" Simpson and nine-year-old James Hanover Thompson with rape for being kissed by a white girl their age on their cheeks in a neighborhood game. The police arrested and sentenced them to reform school where they were to remain until age 21, the remainder of their adolescence. While the boys were incarcerated, the KKK mob and "apron wearing" straight from their kitchen parents of the girl were outside calling for blood on Halloween night.

[Included are Some details of THE CASE: On this date, October 28, 1958, two Black boys, 7-year-old James Hanover Thompson, and 9-year-old David "Fuzzy" Simpson, were among a group of children in Monroe, North Carolina, none more than 10, none younger than 6, playing as young children do without much pattern or apparent direction. Most of the children were white.

One of the girls, Sissy Sutton, kissed Hanover on the cheek. When her mother overheard her relaying the day's events to her sister, she became livid. She called the other white parents, armed herself, gathered some friends, and went out looking for the boys. She intended to kill them.

Mrs. Sutton went to Hanover's home with her posse, not only to kill the boys but to lynch the mothers (lynch mob mentality). They arrived almost at the same time as six carloads of police -- nearly the entire police force of Monroe. Fortunately, no one was at home.

Later that afternoon, a squad car spotted the two boys pulling a little red wagon filled with pop bottles. The police jumped from the car, guns drawn, snatched the boys, handcuffed them, and threw them into the car. One of the policemen slapped Hanover, the first of many beatings he would endure.

When the boys were carried to the jail, they were beaten unmercifully. They were held without counsel and their mothers were not allowed to see them.

For several nights the mothers of the boys were so frightened that they didn't sleep in their own house. Gunmen in passing cars fired dozens of shots into the Thompson home. They killed Hanover's dog. Both women were fired from their jobs as housekeepers. Mrs. Thompson was evicted from her home.

The Klan held daily demonstrations outside of the jail.

On November 4, 1958, six days after taking the boys into custody, local authorities finally held a hearing. The boys had still not seen their parents, friends, or legal counsel. At the hearing, the judge found the boys guilty of three charges of assault (kissing) and molestation. He ordered that the boys be incarcerated in an adult facility for black prisoners, and told the boys that if they behaved, they might be released at age 21.

The national and state NAACP didn't want anything to do with the 'sex case' as Roy Wilkins, head of the national NAACP called it.

Eventually, Robert Franklin Williams civil rights activist whose armed self-defense and shoot out with the local KKK, stopped Klan raids in Monroe, once again PUT HIS LIVE ON THE LINE; he called

New York Civil Rights lawyer Conrad Lynn. The local judge told Lynn that he had had a "separate but equal" hearing. Mrs. Sutton and her daughter made a statement in the morning. That afternoon he summoned the mothers of the two boys and told them that the boys were guilty and were being sent to prison.

As a result of Robert Williams's call to the New York Civil Rights lawyer Conrad Lynn, consequently, Joyce Egginton, a friend of Lynn's and a reporter for the London News-Chronicle, traveled to Monroe. Egginton sneaked into the prison where the boys were held, under the pretense of being a social worker. She also sneaked in a camera. On December 15, 1958, a front page picture of Hanover and Fuzzy in the reformatory, along with an article, appeared all over Europe.

News organizations in England, Germany, Italy, France, Belgium, Spain, all carried the story. The United States Information Agency received more than 12,000 letters expressing outrage at the events.

An international committee was formed in Europe to defend Thompson and Simpson. Huge demonstrations were held in Paris, Rome and Vienna and in Rotterdam against the United States. The U.S. Embassy in Brussels was stoned. It was an international embarrassment for the U.S. government.

As a result of the Robert F. Williams audacity to intervene, in February, North Carolina officials asked the boys' mothers to sign a waiver with the assurance that their children would be released. The mothers refused to sign the waiver, which would have required the boys to admit to being guilty of the charges.

Two days later, after the boys had spent three months in prison, a gubernatorial pardon was granted for Thompson and Simpson without conditions or explanation. The state and city never apologized to the boys or their families for their treatment].

Common human decency and human treatment in the South, during Jim Crow Law was literally unheard of. If a white man said "you done it"—"then by god you done it." During this era, in the South, Black men had no legal rights nor protection under the law without heroes such as Robert F. Williams, a man of unfathomable intellect and a genuine desire for justice in the face of danger.

Chapter 10 The KKK Vowed to kill the Political Mastermind

It usually followed, that when the Klan held a huge rally, they routinely practiced follow-up additional terrorist methods. Even members of the Ladies' Auxiliary of the United Klans of America, Inc., hold their young daughters, also robed in a Klan suit, at a Ku Klux Klan rally in Atlanta on June 5, 1965 with 600 persons in attendance. And only six years earlier in 1959 when they drove the large heavily armed motorcade to Dr. Perry's home while firing their guns at his house, it was the very act of armed self-reliance that sent Catfish Cole's Klan scrambling for their very own lives when they were met with Robert Franklin Williams and his men who drove the Klan off.

But Williams is noteworthy for his "lack" of revolutionary eagerness, that is at the onset—before it came to his realization that the Constitutional Law did not protect the Negro. Early on, Williams was cautious to constantly maintain that the Black Armed Guard was not a defiant and refractory organization, but one dedicated to providing defense to a group of victims, for instance, vulnerable Black people, especially

Black women, who were under attack on a daily and nightly basis and lacking in normal legal remedies: Damages aim at making up the harm that a breaching party (Scapegoats) has committed to the victims; the tendency to blame someone else for one's own problems, a process that often results in feelings of prejudice toward the person or group that one is blaming.

However, until the formation of Williams's Black Armed Guard, Klan night riding and their crimes committed against innocent women during the dark miraculously came to a "instantaneous" stop in Monroe when the Klan experienced weapons firing at them, they suddenly realized they too could "DEPART THIS LIFE!"

This famous incident of Robert Williams' and his men's shrewd positioning of power and control which astounded so many black people—was completely suppressed in the infographics of the time: *Enquirer*; *Times*; *Tribune*; *USA*; *Post*; *Philadelphia/Daily News*; *Herald*; etc. Only Black publications such as *Jet Magazine*, the *Afro-American* the *Norfolk Journal* and *Guide* reported the event of how Williams and his men mystified and out maneuvered the Ku Klux Klan!

Unlike the magnanimous Lumbee victory that sent Catfish Cole and his Klansmen one

Friday night in Robeson County scrambling to flee from more than five hundred rifles and shotguns, Cole's intention was to speak against racial mixing and loose moral behavior of a Lumbee woman who allegedly was having an affair with a white man. As a warning a cross was burned on the Lumbee female's lawn. When the news spread that eastern North Carolina's Hollywood star Eva Gardner was in a relationship with Sammy Davis Jr., who Cole scornfully described as that "one-eyed nigger," Cole was in "mad dog" salivation.

At Maxton, a town in Robeson County, the Klan was to remind the Indians of "their place" in the racial order. The head of the Lumbee chapter Simeon Oxendine, WWII flyer in the fight against the Germans, and Veteran of Foreign Wars response was "We'll just see about that."

Cole had been warned that his life would be in danger if he went to fight in Maxton—if he made those provocative speeches, he had been making about racial mixing and racial purity. During the battle with the Indians, hundreds of Indians let out a thunderous firing of weapons repeatedly in the air. The Klansmen dropped their guns and scrambled for their cars, abandoning the premises and their paraphernalia, allowing the white supremacist to escape. The war organization—the grand wizard himself had abandoned "white womanhood" and fled on foot. The warring Indians even had to help push Catfish Cole's Cadillac out of the ditch where his wife, Carolyn had driven in her attempt to escape to safety.

In a remark by Oxendine, "If the Negroes had done something like this a long time ago, we wouldn't be bothered with the KKK." His remark was in reference to "armed-self-defense!"

Although African American Robert F. Williams and his armed guard had given the hooded men a similar "scramble to safety" just a few weeks before the Indian victory, again, the white media, all had ignored the Monroe NAACP' victorious conflict with the Ku Klux Klan.

****

Ironically, The results of the battle between the Native Americans at Maxton and Catfish Cole landed the "so called wizard" a jail sentence by governor Luther Hodges for preaching racial hatred and inciting a riot. Inasmuch as Williams' newly found combat tactics to defend innocent African Americans prevailed, the damaging and detrimental tactics inflicted on Black victims continued and worsened.

****

Detrimental tactics against Blacks got worse when in the Medlin case a white man attempted to rape a pregnant black woman ended in the judge's decision to drop the charges claiming, "The man was just having a little fun." According to the wife of Robert Franklin Williams, the late Mabel Williams in her report, she stated, "Black women were in tears and wanting to do something." She declared, "such a decision declared 'open season' upon helpless black women in Monroe."

The defenseless black people turned to Robert F. Williams to ask, "What are you going to do now?" Here I refer to him as "The political mastermind"! In a press conference, consequently, Robert Franklin Williams courageously declared one of the most powerful statements of a Black man's lifetime! "If the courts and the Constitution won't protect us, then we must be willing to fight and die for our equal rights and our own protection!"(Williams, Robert F. 1960).

North Carolina authorities were determined to get rid of Robert Franklin Williams because he represented a movement for civil rights.

Robert Williams was then offered bribes by city officials. When that didn't work, they tried to kill him.

One method the whites employed to kill Williams was by automobile accident. On June 23, 1961, Bynum Griffin, the owner of a local car dealership, tried to run Williams and some of his followers off the road. Williams and his followers courageously met their vicious attackers with rifles pointing at them. One white man fell to his knees and cried, "What is this world coming to? The "GD" *niggers* have got guns and the police can't even arrest them." These life threatening events enacted against Williams inspired his written work entitled, **Negroes With Guns**, in 1962.

Anger over a failed attempt to kill Robert F. Williams, caused On Aug. 27, 1961, the full-scale assault launched upon the entire Monroe's Black community. The racists assaulted--beat and jailed "Freedom Riders" -- demonstrators who had come from the North to help overturn segregation.

Chapter 11 An excerpt from the novel Green: Epilogue, 2017

In the late nineteen fifties when the country was becoming aware of my cousin, Robert Franklin Williams, the local NAACP president, and Civil Rights activist, I had just embarked upon the beginning of my teenage years.

Emilee, a pre-teen and our protagonist in the novel, could not have fully understood, at such a young age, the magnitude of the civil rights struggle for blacks in the South, and in her environment. I wrote the novel, to shed light on the historical episodical story told from the young eleven year old's point of view because there is a need for stories to be told from the young female perspective of the tumultuous civil rights era for our readers.

It wasn't until I was a student, living on the west coast, and matriculating at California State University at Northridge in the mid-70s, when I became a part of the camaraderie of the Black Students' Union that was partly organized by Professor W. Burwell, that I discovered the book written by my cousin, Robert Franklin Williams entitled**, Negroes with Guns**.

When I returned to North Carolina in the late 70s, and began a school teaching career, I also began to take writing seriously. I wrote this second novel entitled **Green**, 2017.

I additionally, took an enduring interest in the life of Robert Franklin Williams, firstly, because I had read his book in college, so I knew he was an important man with a commitment to freedom, justice and civil rights; secondly, I took an interest because I was a member of the "kinfolk" at our family reunions where we intermingled with all the members and exchanged ideas with Robert Williams, his wife Mabel, his son Reverend John Williams, and his brother John Herman Williams. My interest was heightened lastly, because I honored him and was in awe with what he stood for - equality, and self-respect, self-determination. He was a man who overcame overwhelming obstacles in life in his brave fight for social justice for the common man. After all, he escaped being lynched, a brilliant and miraculous feat, during the Jim Crow racist era of the South in the 60s.

I could identify with him incredibly because, I myself, overcame so many obstacles in life to where I am today, from first writing my previous five books and now writing *Audacity: Story of a Legendary Hero*. In some ways our lives parallel because to overcome, I first had to save *my own life* at a young age (This story is told in my first book entitled *Emily's Blues, 2016*), and, I believe our life experiences in some respects parallel because it was necessary for me to defy an unjust law to educate *my* mind—I share my story in this discourse because again the analysis and application of Kohlberg's moral development once again may apply. Let it be acknowledged however, that although *I* suffered risk and dangers, my experiences did not parallel to the degree of Mr. Williams' detrimental encounters and hardships].

Chapter 12 Lawrence Kohlberg Analysis and Emily

In this phase, to take this historical narrative and presentation to an advanced level, to better understand Robert Franklin Williams' thought processes, I endeavor to apply the "highest levels of intellectual development" to Williams' decision-making processes (Kohlberg 1981), and measures of "Morality and Racial Identity Development" (Cross et al 1990); ..."African American Child".... (Harris et al 2007) applied to Robert Franklin Williams' mode of moral thinking. In furthering the systematic investigation, I take a risk, as in any project, and apply the subject matter of "scapegoat psychology" to theorize about the actions of "shadow collectives," mass violent destructive acts of the 50s and 60s perpetrated against victims representing social and racial variations— minorities (Neumann 1969).

The organizers of the venue LYNCHING WITHOUT SANCTUARY, October 11-13, 2012 at the Levine Museum of the New South and the University of North Carolina at Charlotte Center City offer the registered attendees the opportunity to witness this broad range of disciplines and the impact of lynching past, present and prevalent. Then those attending may come away with the resolve of connectedness in a continuing struggle for the rights of all humans. More importantly, that we should not forget our past for it is the means to expand our ties for an improved interdependent future.

According to Cornel West, "...you can have the most sophisticated and acute analysis of power in the world, but if you don't have compassion in your soul and love in your heart, you are still going to end up with a movement that cannot touch people at the deepest level and in the end, reproduce structures of domination that are unaccounted for with those leaders who claim to be speaking on behalf of common folk" (2).

Relevant to the before mentioned mode of moral thinking, psychology as a subject, deals with the human mind and behavior, which makes it one of the most extensively, studied subjects. Why? It helps us to get an insight into the human psyche and behavior patterns; and my analysis leads me to believe it helps us understand why Robert Franklin Williams had to take such drastic measures, self-defense and civil disobedience; risking his life to unselfishly protect his people, his family and his own life.

The subject of moral development (what is right, what is wrong and the reasoning behind it) generates interest here because it is one of the most basic forms of behavior to which every human being can relate. " It reflects a distinctly human ability to engage in higher order cognition and reflects the values, norms, and social mores of society." This is where Lawrence Kohlberg's moral development and his stage theory of justice and rights may apply.

Kohlberg became famous for his work as a professor at Harvard University beginning in the early 1970s. He started as a developmental psychologist and then moved to the field of moral education, popularizing his findings through research studies conducted at Harvard's Center for Moral Education (Barger 2000).

While some argue, the Kohlberg study is limited (Rest 1979), it is understandable because his studies did not adequately represent the moral situations that many children and adolescents such as young Robert Franklin Williams encountered in everyday experiences involving racial discrimination in the 50s and 60s in the towns like Monroe, North Carolina.

Rest (1979), for example, claims that some participants were moving backward in stages. However, since Kohlberg considers cognitive development as related to moral development, he claims that the more cognitive development increases, the greater the moral development. However, it provides examples of how victims of discrimination utilized different ways of processing moral predicaments (Harris 138). e.g., predicaments such as violent burning of crosses in the yards of blacks, bombing their homes; beating and raping of black women, shootings, white supremacists' fear tactics mob violence—lynch politics.

Kohlberg's theory of moral development was dependent on the thinking of the Swiss psychologist Jean Piaget and the American philosopher John Dewey. He was also inspired by James Mark Baldwin. These men had emphasized that human beings develop philosophically and psychologically in a progressive fashion. Kohlberg believed...and was able to demonstrate through studies...that people progressed in their moral reasoning (i.e., in their basis for ethical behavior) through a series of stages. He believed that there were six identifiable stages which could be more generally classified into three levels. The Heinz dilemma used as one of the main examples in psychology was based on a situation that was introduced to a group of young male students and their responses related to moral development thus checked.

Heinz had a wife who was on her death bed because of being afflicted by a certain cancer form. A special radium that was recently discovered by a druggist of the same town was touted to save her. So, Heinz ordered the drug, which costs $200 to be manufactured, but the druggist quoted the price at $2000. Heinz could not afford the drug and pleaded to the druggist to sell it for less because his wife was on her deathbed. But the druggist refused.

In desperation, Heinz stole the drug.

The boys were then questioned about whether what Heinz did was right or wrong, thus helping to study the reasoning behind those answers which acted as moral dilemmas for students. The following are the 6 stages that he drew from:

Level 1: Preconventional Morality

<u>Stage 1</u> (Obedience and Punishment) ~ In this stage, rules are looked upon as being absolute and fixed and are followed with the objective of avoiding punishments. People behave according to socially acceptable norms because they are told to do so by some authority figure (i.e., parent or teacher)

<u>Stage 2</u> (Individualism and Exchange) ~ In this stage, the rules are given secondary importance and what is focused on instead is the way in which individual needs are satisfied. This level is characterized by a view that right behavior means acting in one's own best interest.

Level 2: Conventional Morality

<u>Stage 3</u> (Interpersonal Relationships) ~ Conforming to societal rules become important. Decisions are based with the view of how they affect others. 'Good Boy-Nice Girl Orientation'

attitudes which seek to do what will gain the approval of others.

Stage 4 (Maintaining 'Law and Order' Social Order) ~ 'Society' as a concept becomes clearer. They learn to be a part of the same by following societal rules and law and responding to the obligations of duties that are expected of them.

Level 3: Postconventional Morality

Stage 5 (Social Contract and Individual Rights) ~ The differing values, beliefs and opinions of the other members of society come to the forefront. Maintaining of law with differing personalities and a genuine interest in the welfare of others poses a challenge as Kohlberg felt, interestingly enough, is not reached by the majority of adults.

Stage 6 (Universal Ethical Principles) ~ Respect for universal principles and the demands of individual conscience. People follow their individual sets of rules and values, even though they clash with societal rules and principles.

This belief based on the stages of moral development as theorized by Kohlberg, gives us some understanding of how moral behavior is developed throughout the lifespan--even beginning at a young age as in the case of young Robert Franklin Williams's experiences. It is very interesting to note that the value system and moral behavior which includes ethics and morality is dimensional, thus it can be studied and theorized upon in comparison with the important values in society. If we look at the values of human life and how Robert Williams demonstrated that he believed it should be protected. It gives us an understanding of how the human mind and psyche develop cognitively and physically in response to physiological aging, psychosocial interactions, and environmental situations. Rujuta Borkar: 2-18-2011.

Kohlberg believed that individuals could only progress through these stages one stage at a time. That is, ***they could not "jump" stages. They could not, for example, move from an orientation of selfishness to the law and order stage without passing through the good boy/girl stage. They could only come to a comprehension of a moral rationale one stage above their own. Thus, according to Kohlberg, it was important to present them with moral dilemmas for discussion which would help them to see the reasonableness of a "higher stage" morality and encourage their development in that direction (Clark, F; Chilton, S).

****

[Yet, prior to the analysis of Robert Franklin Williams' mode of thinking, I now include "The Story of Emily" and Kohlberg's theory. As it should lead us into a parallel of related modes of thinking between Emily's and Robert F. Williams. This modality of thinking should illustrate the premise of Quality of Life over Blind Obedience to the Law.

Emily was the mother of five children, whose husband had been incarcerated. Emily was receiving AFDC, Aide to Dependent Children. Emily had put herself through high school, and she desired a four-year college education which she knew her family could not provide. Emily felt and believed she had a right to an education—a right that has been handed down to us in the Declaration of Independence and the Bill of Rights. The right to Life, Liberty and Pursuit of Happiness. These are ideals that the American citizens find their government would fight for. Emily had a desire to change the quality of life for her children and herself. In explicating her desire and condition to the "Case Worker", she was advised that there was a one-year funding program. She enrolled into Los Angeles Trade Tech College; one year later Emily graduated from Secretarial/Stenography school with a one year completion certificate.

She was in a hurry to get a well-paying job. Emily soon discovered that to get a well-paying job, one must have a good education—which meant a four-year-degree.

Emily returned to the "Case Worker", explicated her discovery, and expressed a desire to return to school as an English major. Dropping her eyeglasses, the "Case Worker" informed Emily that this idea was absolutely 'UNREAL.' The agency further informed Emily that if she did not continue her job, the AFDC funds would be discontinued.

Emily, being a self-actualized person, and one who knew her validity even at an early age, innately knew that she possessed the intellect to achieve in school, if given the opportunity. But could she sacrifice the income needed to sustain the basic deficiency needs for her children and herself. She certainly could not. Then, the only other way would be to defy the law.

Emily resigned from her menial paying typist job, and enrolled into Los Angeles Valley Junior College, at Van Nuys while receiving AFDC. She qualified for financial aid from the college program. Let it be noted, that as a student at LAVJC she became a Dean's List student and was endorsed by the Tia Alpha Epsilon sorority with an invitation to join as recognition of her high achievement.

Emily knew that eventually she would have to face the consequences of her actions, but she was acting according to a higher principle—a right to an education and an improved lifestyle.

She moved into action: She researched the philosophies of the Welfare Program, which proved to be one of "Betterment for the Social Institution of the Family." Emily was fighting for the betterment of life and mind, providing a role model for herself and her children, which eventually, and hopefully would provide an improved family income.

Emily's Reasoning: Stage 5 and 6 of the Kohlberg Moral Development Level

Emily like her cousin Robert Franklin Williams had a strong sense of law and respect for authority. Her lineage was a strong background of two working parents, Jones and Lillie Williams, who adhered to the laws. She valued education, having been exposed to successful, and educated individuals upon who she modeled herself and her lifestyle.

She believed in constructive use of the Welfare Program.

Emily also believed as Martin Luther King Jr. for example, that laws are valid insofar as they are grounded in justice, and that a commitment to justice carries with it an obligation to disobey unjust laws: Stage 6 thinking.

Emily felt that a law which denied her the right to an education, on the basis of finances, when there indeed were funds available in the financial programs, was considered an unjust law—this can be paralleled with changing or improving the quality of one's life. Emily wanted her actions to call attention to the philosophy of the Welfare System. Ideally the system indorsed "Betterment", but in reality, it seemed that it did not.

In an attempt to get a better understanding, and paraphrase what Kohlberg says, we proceed to a just decision by viewing a situation through the eyes of others. Therefore, the "veil of ignorance", acting as if one's role is unknown, will be assumed. From the point of view of the AFDC "Case Worker" – Emily's actions would be a clear cut and dry case of Stage 4 thinking—Level 2, Conventional Level— violation of the law. Further, society's view (perhaps the courts during that era late 60s) would perpetrate and support the views of the "Case Worker."

In conclusion, Emily did call attention to the unjust law: An individual cannot receive AFDC while receiving financial aid. There was a hearing—and the ruling was in favor of the plaintiff.

Emily was granted the right to attend college and receive both grants, academic and AFDC. Four years later, Emily graduated from California State University at Northridge with a Degree in English.

Kohlberg explains it this way: the Constitution is based on a Stage 5 morality—basic human rights—life, liberty and the dignity of the individual. The Declaration of Independence, another Stage 5 document says: We hold these truths to be self-evident, that all men are created equal, that they are endowed by the Creator with certain unalienable rights that cannot be given nor taken away; the right to life, liberty and the pursuit of happiness.... That whenever any form of government becomes destructive of these ends, it is the right of the people to alter or to abolish it...(Kohlberg 1978).

In the "Story of Emily", her thinking emerged out of a moral dilemma of what society should value. Her mode of reasoning was concerned with self-chosen ethical principles—universal principles of justice, equality of human rights, and respect for dignity of human being as individual persons—Level III, Post-conventional level, considered by Kohlberg to be the highest level].

Chapter 13 To resume the excerpt from the Epilogue of Green

[In the story of Robert Franklin Williams: At one family reunion in 1984, I had the privilege and pleasure of interviewing Robert Franklin Williams, who spoke honestly and candidly about some of his life experiences as the president of the NAACP in Monroe, North Carolina and living abroad in Cuba and China.

During my teaching career, 1979-2014, I researched and collected an abundance of provocative materials about Mr. Williams. And it was in 2012 that I proposed an idea to the "Lynching without Sanctuary" Conference committee at the University of North Carolina at Charlotte, where I taught English Rhetoric and Composition. My proposal was accepted. In completing this research, I consulted with the late Reverend John Williams, son of Robert F. Williams, who instantaneously gave me his blessings and approval and continued, effortlessly, to communicate with me until the research was completed.

During the year of the race riot in Monroe (referred to as Morris Town in the novel) I was living in either, Monroe, Washington, DC or

Brooklyn, New York and returning to my hometown for short intervals.

The following is a researched account of some of the events based on actual occurrences; referred to in the story **GREEN**.

The reporter says, "Whites chased RW and a carload of Negroes down the highway after they and some Freedom Riders picketed the "whites only" swimming pool, and when their car was finally forced off the road and came to a stop, white men carrying guns surrounded it. RW and his followers jumped out of his car unexpectedly with their guns, and suddenly gunshots were exchanged, which made the Whites run away in fear for their own safety. One white man fell to the ground openly, loudly weeping calling Williams and his men "GD niggers!" over the sight of what he was seeing: Black men with their weapons ready to protect themselves against white attackers after the automobile they were riding in being forced off the road.

Later on, in Bright Town, a riot develops; gun warfare of black and white citizens and the police outbreak in front of the courthouse square and in Bright Town sent some blacks running for their lives after being shot at by white men wearing police uniforms. This went on downtown, on the railroad tracks, and the streets.

Demonstrators were shot, imprisoned without medical attention. Once in jail, they were brutally beaten by white cellmates, receiving broken ribs and severe head injuries.

A white rampage combed through the black community. RW supporters armed themselves with shotguns, semiautomatic military carbines and went downtown to try to save the picketers, where they were met with armed guns pointing and firing at them. A horrible gun battle caused a police officer to get hit with a bullet in his thigh. The black men had to run back to Bright Town on foot.

Carloads of Klan racists roamed through the city all night, attacking blacks and some whites they called liberal whites. The Klan shot through houses. The Bright Town Journal article said, "A bloody racial war went on. Black people in droves ran to Bright Town, barely escaping mob-hooded white attackers."

Hundreds of blacks formed at RW's house in Bright Town, many of them armed. They feared the jailed people would not survive the night. Some angry blacks talked of killing white people. RW's aim was to settle the crowd and keep them from danger. Controlling the battered and frightened citizens was extremely challenging, however, as members of the NAACP, they finally responded to RW in a disciplined and organized manner. It was necessary to barricade certain streets, mainly Tobye Street, posting young followers who positioned themselves in trees along Winchester Avenue. Young men stood guard with guns on porches. They set up effective defense perimeters. Speaking calmly with authority, RW told black men, "If the Klan rides and tries to do wrong against you, stop them, protect your family, and your home. The weapons are not for killing. Killing is wrong." The outbreak of violence prompted state troopers. Governor Terry Sanford's office intervened, but had to keep a safe distance from RW's barricaded perimeters and keep the whites from there. News of violence spread to other parts of the country. People were calling from the county and the country about their sons and daughters. RW, who had formed allies around the county and the country, was constantly on the telephone. When a white couple, reportedly, drove in into the black neighborhood, their car was surrounded, and they were pulled out. RW heard the unrest in the streets and came out. Williams is said to have ordered his followers not to attack them and to have ushered the couple into his Toby Street home for safety against the angry wishes of the agitated crowd. The couple was lodged in Mr.

Williams' home until later that night when they could leave the neighborhood safely. They later report to the authorities that they were "being surrounded by "niggers.""

While Williams once again risked his life to save even the white couple who practiced separatism and who obviously had driven into the Black angry mod during the Monroe uprising, the Monroe authorities used this which later became the basis of an alleged abduction charge. Consequently, the federal and state government issued an FBI Most Wanted warrant, citing RW as **Armed and Extremely Dangerous.** Additionally, to the safety of the white couple he saved, was another main concern-- the fate of the innocent protesters, who were still behind bars in the downtown jail. However, the sequence of events that unfolded prevented Williams from enacting safety measures for the protesters. That night the police chief called Mr. Williams and promised to send state troopers.

Void of any protection of Constitutional Law, **Robert Williams was forced to make a decision to avoid being lynched.**

Chapter 14 Robert F. Williams and Lawrence Kohlberg Analysis: Quality of Life vs Blind Obedience of Law

In this phase of the narrative, *Audacity Story of a Legendary Hero,* I now apply, as previously stated the Quality of Life over Blind Obedience of Law—Constructive Use of Defiance and Civil Disobedience as they relate to Robert Franklin Williams' thinking and his effort to "stand up" for his oppressed people. Robert F. Williams fought against Kangaroo Courts functioning under the influence of Jim Crow in the 50s and 60s. The focus will be placed upon Lawrence Kohlberg's Level III, Post conventional autonomous, of principled level.

There is a clear effort to define moral values and principles that have validity and application apart from the authority. This level has two stages: Stages 5 and Stage 6 of moral development. It is believed and set out to tell the story, of how they helped motivate Robert Franklin Williams' mode of reasoning as a young boy. Evidence shows it was his ability to apply abstract reasoning to social issues of the day. The unjust laws imposed by Jim Crow inadvertently influenced the ethical principles instilled in his psyche at the "right time" espoused by his parents during his young life that prevailed and caused him to make an important decision to be different. We see a cause and effect scenario: Cause: his choice to be different from the defenseless Black men as he had witnessed their inability to "fight" for their rights—Effect: this "right" behavior prevailed on into adulthood, which inevitable self-defense and the defense of many others saved lives, including, his wife and two sons, and many others i.e., community dwellers, Freedom Riders; Mr. and Mrs. Stegall; Dr. Perry and his family, and the two innocent boys who almost loss their lives after being accused of getting kissed by a young white female.

To expound upon this premise, Stage 5, The Social Contract, Legalistic Orientation: Here the idea is organization v morality. Respondents basically believe that a good society is best conceived as a social contract into which people enter into freely to work toward the benefit of all. Recognition is given to the fact that different social groups within a society will have different values, BUT they would agree on two points—basic rights, as life and liberty to be protected, and the democratic procedures for changing unfair laws and improving society.

The subject of stage 5 is basically one of morality and their mode of reasoning. At Stage 5 people are making more of an independent effort to think out *what society should value.* For example, a clear case in point, if we view the actions taken by our historian *Ms. Rosa Parks* and her refusal to give up her seat on the Montgomery Alabama bus to a white man, we see an independent effort to think out what society should value—the right to choose where to sit on the public bus irrelevant to skin pigmentation.

Stage 6, Universal Principles, respondents are defining the principles of which agreements will be most just. It concerns one's *decision of conscious* in accord with self-chosen ethical principles—universal principles of justice, equality of human rights, and respect for the dignity of human beings as individual persons (Kohlberg 1978).

I hope I'm not getting ahead of myself here, but I must acknowledge the fact that before Martin Luther King Jr., before Malcolm X, before the Black Panthers, there was Robert Franklin Williams. I cannot resist the need to apply the actions of young Robert Franklin Williams, the first African American civil rights leader to advocate and demonstrate armed resistance to racial oppression and violence and his drastic decision to organize even as a young boy/leader who demonstrated "black power' to deter those white philanders lurking through the dark streets of the Monroe neighborhood seeking local black women for sex. And because it is such an important detail, it will be alluded to throughout this segment of the Robert Franklin Williams' narrative.

Human rights and the quality of life should prevail over blind obedience of an unjust law. As this discourse should reveal Robert Franklin Williams motivations grew out of a need for quality of human life over blind obedience of—unfair law—

unjust law—violations to the United States Constitution. It is important to point out--his mode of thinking develops out of a strong sense of self pride instilled within him from family upbringing and a moral problem. Although Kohlberg maintains that the stages are not the product of socialization, (e.g., parents and teachers). But that they emerge, again, from stimulation of our mental processes through discussions and questioning (Kohlberg 1981).

To differ from Kohlberg on this point, it is maintained that Robert Franklin Williams thinking emerged from ***exigency*** in the form of the Negro community problem in Monroe, North Carolina. The violence acted upon unprotected citizens once we examine the connection between morality and Black racial identity (Harris 145). At one instance in 1961, Chief Mauney, of the Monroe, NC police threatened Robert Franklin Williams with these words: "In thirty minutes you'll be hanging from a tree in the courthouse square."

But Williams wasn't lynched-- not because the threat wasn't real, not because he assumed a passive reaction, on the contrary, because of his active morality to the threat. Williams' audacity to use his own power primarily for his own benefit as any normal human being would. Williams resorted to the use of his own power to oppose community violence acted upon unprotected citizens like himself. Similar expressions of agency caused runaway enslaved person to be beaten—killed. It caused Black-Wall Street to become burned to the ground in 1921; and it's what caused black leaders' death (modern day forms of lynching) during the 60s. This violence continues to cause unjustifiable deaths of young black males killed today in the twenty-first century: Trayvon Martin was an unarmed American 17-year-old killed by George Zimmerman on February 26, 2012, sparking a national controversy. There were eight Unarmed Black Males other than **Trayvon Martin** who were recently **killed**. At sixteen years old, Kimani Gray on his way home from a birthday party was shot to **death** by **two plainclothes officers** in Brooklyn; Eric Garner was killed in a chokehold by NYPD; Dontre Hamilton was killed in Milwaukee; John Crawford III, age 22, Dayton, Ohio killed, officer not charged. 18 year old Michael Brown Jr. was shot six time and the police were not charged. Let us be reminded of the recent choking death of the victim George Floyd for allegedly passing a counterfeit twenty dollar bill at a convenience store.

To refer once again to the Heinz dilemma, Robert F. Williams' mental ability generated a course of action to save his own "skin." For example, in the story of "Heinz steals the Drug," a dilemma which establishes a basis for discussion and reasoning. In contrast to Kohlberg's dilemma, a study conducted by Yvette R. Harris and James A. Graham asks, "What if Heinz Were Black?" (133). According to Concepts in African-Centered Psychology "Theories of African American personality: Basic Constructs and Empirical

Predictions/ Assessment, (7 Kambon et al 2012), AA personality as driven by the same Eurocentric motivational forces as White Americans, such as achievement driven, individualism, materialism and power-dominance driven, assertiveness-aggression as optimal motivation, along with an emphasis on differences, competitiveness, violence, victory-driven, conflict, strife, anxiety avoidance, shame and guilt all as critical psychological elements in "normal personality operation" (Azibo, 1990; Kambon, 1992, 1998).

Chapter 15 His Faith of Civil Law is Undermined

Robert Franklin Williams was an American civil rights leader and author best known for serving as president of the Monroe, North Carolina chapter of the NAACP in the 1950s and into 1961. Additionally, he succeeded in integrating the local public library and swimming pool in Monroe at a time of high racial tension and official abuses. His firsthand experience with lawlessness and white supremacy, the unprotected and alienated occurrences from the police and the justice system under minded his faith in civil law during his childhood, indisputably influenced his views of self-defense and direct action.

The social experience regarding wrongness, relating to the story he would eventually retell throughout his life, which began at an early age of eleven in 1936. The ideas of wrongness toward human lives penetrated Robert Williams's thought processes based upon what he continued to see happening to his helpless people: rape, brutalization, house burning, lynching, shootings-- complete lawlessness related to African Americans in his hometown. I maintain that this social experience challenged his ideas regarding punishment, injustice and disobedience (Kohlberg 24).

To provide more details surrounding Williams' psyche, as a child departing his home with good thoughts at the tender age of eleven following a prayer meeting on a Friday night at his home where he was raised with two loving parents, John and Emma Williams, young Robert responded to his mother, Emma Williams' request to go to the downtown post office on Main Street in Monroe. With the Negro spiritual "What a Friend We have in Jesus" still resonating in his mind, as he approached the courthouse directly at the square; Williams at such a delicate age, witnessed and observed this horrific act: a black woman dragged with her dress over her buttock and beaten by the police chief of Monroe, Jesse Helms, Sr., the father of the U.S. Senator Jesse Helms Jr., "U.S. Senator Jesse Helms, who made a career on inciting race prejudice by slandering black people" (Tyson 2019).

Level II. Conventional Morality: Stage 3. At this stage children—who are now entering their teens—see morality as more than simple deals. They believe that people should live up to the expectations of the family and community and behave in "good" ways (Kohlberg 1978).

I have not deliberately chosen this one incident, the witnessed beating of a vulnerable black woman and the helplessness of the black men, who looked on idly: Nevertheless, it clearly emphasizes the defenselessness impressed upon the eleven year old Williams' soul. He was witness to the white Supremacists' act, a clear case of behaving in a lawless "not good" manner—to put it this way, perpetration of "lynch politics" upon a helpless female. More than this, at the core of such an act perpetrated upon this black minority victim—is the destructive unconscious shadow of scapegoat psychology. The unconscious psychic conflicts of massed groups (the collectives) find their most spectacular outlets in epidemic eruptions such as mob violence and or violence perpetrated by individuals supported by the mob (Neumann 49). This white systemic and inhuman, brutal, supremacist dominant impact of black degradation and inferior human worth would astonish Williams' mind and haunt him throughout his life.

At that very point, when Williams vowed to be different, even though he was a child, he stepped into the shoes of a responsible adult—which meant, societal influences caused this young child to grow up fast. We see again, the hand of fate; and we see a case of Level III Stage 5 and 6 thinking: Decision making ability applied at the right time—validity and application apart from authority—an adult decision to "arise." Even as a youth, young Robert Williams knew what he witnessed was not right.

More importantly, simply put—it was wrong in every sense of the word. It certainly appears that his conscience would not allow him to rest soundlessly at night in his bed with the knowledge of this brutal act perpetrated upon this helpless Black woman with no human recourse—no person came to her rescue. And he himself, Williams, had to move to action, which led as mentioned previously in this analysis, to do something about it—to put an end to such an atrocious occurrence. He desired to protect this woman, who by the way was symbolic of his sister, his mother, his aunt—a defenseless woman to be protected the very same manner in which the white man protected their womenfolk.

His movements subsequently caused Robert Franklin Williams to face supremist racists' desire to hang him.

John Williams, Robert's father would occasionally take his son to Seaboard Rail line where he worked as a boiler washer, considered the highest skilled position a black man could hold during this era and location. Young Robert observed the racial politics of the railroad yard work although railroad work provided employment that did not depend entirely on the local white power structure (Williams 5-6). At his father's place of employment, he heard white men talk of their attraction to black women; the power of white skin as "deliberate humiliation" to black men. As previously stated, young Robert's initial experience with violence and white supremacy during his childhood certainly influenced his vision of self-protection and direct action. Once again, we visualize Robert Williams growing up fast. When Robert Williams made a conscious decision to defy the law, organizing the secret group with friends "to make war on white philanders who practiced a double standard—humiliation for the black woman in daylight but who fancied black women after dark, this was Williams' first direct confrontation with white supremacy. Williams used defiance at this early age as protection--to protect black citizens from the exploitation and degradation of whites. A clear example of the hero's choice of civil disobedience—a sense of right and wrong and the idea that laws are valid insofar as they are grounded in justice, and that a commitment to justice carries with it an obligation to disobey unjust laws—a law that did not protect humans on the basis of the color of their skin--***pigmentation*** a point elaborated upon earlier: Stage 6 thinking (Kohlberg 1981).

****

Chapter 16 KKK Intimidation: Rocks, Bottles, Pistols Fired

Clearly to the mind and eyes, now we see the man Robert Franklin Williams manifest: When by 1955 the NAACP chapter in Monroe had dwindled down to six members. And in a series of twenty rallies, beginning in 1956, several Monroe and a dozen more within forty miles, James Catfish Cole led the KKK drawing crowds as many as 15,000 whites. After each rally and cross burning, dozens of carloads of Klansmen rode through the black community of Monroe, blowing their horns, throwing rocks and bottles, and firing pistol shots into the air. Children reared during this time remember how devastating this occurrence was for families—mothers (whose husbands, the fathers of their children were attending a secret self-defense meeting) and the young siblings' fear as the KKK drove down the Black community streets like Fairley Avenue. The Chief of Police Mauney acknowledged to reporters of the

Observer newspaper that he led Ku Klux Klan motorcades through the black community, claiming he maintained order.

****

Using his anti-lynch politics, Williams told his childhood stories to help inspire black citizens that they were men. He went further to share his belief of how, as men there should be a connection to community and racial identity—identify with their Blackness (internalization) not only connection to self, but also a commitment to helping others (within and outside of their racial group to find a solid sense of identity). The Internalization component of racial identity refers to a feeling of inner security about Blackness because one has incorporated the attitudes of the immersion/emersion experience—movement from a negative to a positive self-identity in the context of their racial group membership. "Ideological flexibility and a general decline in strong antiwhite feelings also typify the internalization stage" (Parham & Helms 1990).

He further inspired black citizens to identify with manhood and citizenship when he recruited individuals, domestic working class, farmers, and the unemployed from pool halls, barber shop, street corners and tenant farms. He recruited black veterans, for example, his cousin, the late Jones McConnie Williams, who trained in the use of Army artillery before his station in the Philippines during 1942 WWII. Once more, "children" both male and female at the time, vividly remember the attendance of their father's secret meetings at Dr. Albert Perry's home (the local black doctor who became the object of the KKK's rage and lynch-mob mentality). The doctor's home was designated for the location of the "Guard," the organized group designed to defend themselves with armed self-reliance against the KKK.

Williams announced in the Monroe Enquirer, "All citizens who believe in democracy, the rights of man, and brotherhood are urged to join and support the NAACP. This organization is open to all people, irrespective of race, who support the American cause as embodied in the United States Constitution." Here again we see Robert F. Williams exercising Stage 5 principles: The Social Contract, legalistic Orientation: The idea of organization v morality. Respondents basically believe that a good society is best conceived as a social contract into which people inter into freely to work toward the benefit of all. Recognition is given to the fact that different social groups within a society will have different values, but again, they would agree on two points—to reiterate, they believe in basic rights, as life and liberty to be protected, and the democratic procedures for changing unfair laws and improving society. The subject of stage 5 is basically one of morality and their mode of reasoning. People are making more of an independent effort, such as our hero Robert F. Williams; Ms. Rosa Parks and the Montgomery bus encounter; and Emily (from the 'Story of Emily' experience) to think out what society should value (Kohlberg 1978).

Referring again to the denied swimming pool access to black—"drownings", unfortunately, black children were dying in murky mud holes because they had no safe place to swim. With the drowning death of a young black boy in the summer of 1957, the fight against racism and the consensus among well-meaning whites and blacks began to break. While white children swam at the Monroe Country Club's "Whites Only" swimming pool, built in 1935 with $200,000 in federal funds from the Works Progress Administration and the Parks and Recreation Commission, both as a member of the NAACP and as a representative of the interracial Human Relations Council, met with commissioners who objected "on the grounds that to allow Negroes to swim even once a week would be too expensive because the water would have to be changed after the colored people used it." Following a meeting the chair of the commission Harvey Morrison assured "that he would not recommend that Negroes be allowed to use the pool under any circumstances." White liberals showed no sign of understanding that black children were losing their lives in the unsafe swimming holes.

According to Robert Franklin Williams (Special Collection) almost immediately, Dr. Perry and I led a contingent of eight black youths with bathing suits and towels to the country club swimming pool, where they demanded to swim. Refused admission, we conducted a brief "stand-in" protest near the gate, repeating the process several times. Angry whites immediately drew up a petition "asking that local Negro integrationists be forced to leave Monroe.... The petition was aimed at Robert F. Williams, president, and Dr. A.E. Perry, vice president of the Monroe NAACP."

Robert F. Williams desire to 'do right' by the black youths in Monroe caused him to become unstoppable even with the words and actions of the "grand wizard" resonating in his mind. James's "Catfish" Cole led a KKK revival in nearby Salisbury later told a crowd of 2,000 whites, as alluded to earlier in this discourse, "Those niggers must be ready to meet their maker." (I interpret these words as a sign of the times "looking to be lynched—lynch mob politics, i.e., scapegoat psychology), contents which are capable of becoming conscious but whose access to consciousness has been blocked, become evil and destructive—because of the "shadow" who sees the alien out there rather than seeing "one's own inner problem, which is transferred to the outside world. Therefore "It" is combated, punished and exterminated (Neuman 1969).

Chapter 17 Williams, King and Malcolm

It is evident that Robert Franklin Williams and Martin Luther King Jr. paralleled in their ideas of civil and human rights. For example, Robert F. Williams never spoke against the passive resistance advocated by Minister King who felt Nonviolence is the way of the strong. Nonviolence is not for the cowardly, the weak, the passive, … Principles of Nonviolent Resistance By Martin Luther King Jr. First, it must be emphasized that nonviolent resistance is not a method for cowards; it does resist. If one uses this method because one is afraid or merely because one lacks the instruments of violence, this person is not truly nonviolent. This is why Gandhi often said that if cowardice is the only alternative to violence, it is better to fight.

The goal of nonviolence is redemption and reconciliation; to defeat evil, not people. Nonviolence includes a willingness to accept suffering without retaliation, to accept the blows from the aggressor.

Where feasible, Robert Franklin Williams believed nonviolence should be used acknowledging civil disobedience to be a powerful weapon under "civilized conditions." This is seen in Robert Franklin Williams' nonviolent sit-ins with Freedom Riders during the 60s. However, in contrast to King, Williams' ideology aliened also with Malcolm X who said, "I myself would go for nonviolence if it was consistent, if everybody was going to be nonviolent all the time… If they make the Ku Klux Klan nonviolent, I'll be nonviolent. If they make the White Citizens Council nonviolent, I'll be nonviolent… I don't think it's fair to tell our people to be nonviolent unless someone is out there making the Klan and these other groups also be nonviolent" like the Citizens Council—a loosely organized group to terrorize and intimidate Blacks (Worley et al 1987).

Let it be noted here, in a telephone interview with the late John Chalmer Williams, son of Robert Franklin Williams, he reported, "Although Malcolm X considered Robert F. Williams a forerunner in ideas of armed, self-reliance and anti-lynch politics, strangely enough, contrasted to my father, but Malcolm X rarely took up arms against white attackers" (2015).

Chapter 18   Examination of moral development and the African American male: If Heinz were Black

To comment further on the Heinz dilemma focused upon earlier, it is believed, had this scenario taken place in cities such as Monroe, in North Carolina, in the 50s and 60s, and Heinz were an African American male According to Gilligan, in the study of "Heinz Steals the Drug" it is believed, even in today's twenty-first century, if Heinz were a Black male, many issues would need to be considered in the examination. The story would certainly change and the discourse with the judge would be contextually different. Heinz would have been lynched if there were no hero such as Robert Franklin Williams and his strong belief in human rights and moral decency which evolved from African cultural integrity. Oliver 1989 for Black Heinz related to exigency.

The Emmitt Till incident and the Dr. Martin Luther King Jr. leadership set the stage for Rosa Parks who championed the year-long Montgomery Bus Boycott maintained in reference to Robert Franklin Williams, said: "those who marched with Martin Luther King Jr. in Alabama admired Williams "for his courage and his commitment to freedom. Those who knew Williams believed in "armed self-reliance" and was "a very good friend" of Malcolm X.

Chapter 19 I Will Walk Upright as a Man compels Martin Luther King

As president of the Monroe NAACP in the late 1950s, Williams watched as members of his community were denied basic rights, tormented by the KKK, and ignored in the courts. Seeing no other recourse, fueled by his recognized reach for human decency he continued to advocate "armed self-reliance" in the face of the white terrorism, encouraging members of his NAACP chapter to protect their homes against the Klan with rifles and sandbag fortifications.

In the spring of 1959, Williams was again the subject of national attention when the NAACP suspended him from the presidency of the Monroe chapter because the local chapter had formed a rifle club to protect the nearby black community of Newtown from harm (where the focus of their attention should have been) attacks by whites.

Williams' advocacy for self-reliance made him into an example at the 1959 NAACP convention. He had been removed from his post as Monroe NAACP president, and he listened at the convention as 40 speakers denounced him. He responded that he had called for self-defense, *not acts of war:* **"We as men should stand up as men and protect our women and children.** I am a man, and I will walk upright as a man should. I WILL NOT CRAWL." His logic compelled Martin Luther King, Jr. to acknowledge that, "When the Negro uses force in self-defense, he does not forfeit support -- he may even win it, by the courage and self-respect it reflects."

As the debate over violence and nonviolence raged on, during Williams' suspension, the people in his branch voted to make Mabel, his wife serve in his place. At the end of a six months period, an election was held, and Robert Franklin Williams was unanimously re-elected to the office as the NAACP president. In 1961, and King's announcement of "Freedom Riders" to assist the organization of a nonviolent campaign in Williams' hometown, as stated previously, the white mobs caused the nonviolent crusade in Monroe to disintegrate into a violence uprising.

Ironically, that night, as reported earlier in this narrative, during the Monroe uprising, Williams once again put his life on the line to save the white couple by sheltering them in his home. The city in their search to rid themselves of Williams's civil rights movement once and for all, found their method when they used his benevolent protective actions for the white couple who he had saved. That same night, after the police chief telephoned

Robert Williams and promised, "***In thirty minutes, you'll be hanging from a tree in front of the courthouse,***" after viewing his name and photograph flash across the black and white television screen announcing 'the federal and state government has issued an FBI Most Wanted warrant, citing Mr. Williams as **Armed and Extremely Dangerous**.' At that point Robert Williams realized the limitations of his armed strategies under the circumstances of the Jim Crow law of the South, he and Mabel were forced to flee from Monroe, North Carolina into New York, to Canada then to Cuba to escape the hundreds of FBI agents who combed the countryside for them. One of the agents reported his frustrations to J. Edgar Hoover: "Subject has become something of a 'John Brown' to Negroes around Monroe, and they will do anything for him."

In an interview with me, in 1985 with Robert Franklin Williams, he confessed, "I was once told by the police, 'Your father was a good man and never gave us any trouble.' And I responded, That's why I have to." The trouble he spoke about concerned black pride, human rights and justice, supposedly guaranteed by the US Constitution— the right to life, liberty and the pursuit of happiness- human rights that were being denied to black citizens. Robert Franklin Williams went on to express, "The most trouble you can get into is to try and see that the Constitution applies to all humanity. I believe in self-defense not aggression, but protecting family and myself—never overthrowing the government, but enforcement of the Constitution."

"Freedom; fair trial, justice; these are words that have a different meaning to the white man, and used to deprive Negroes of their basic human rights that the courts uphold as the mad racists are allowed to continue the practice of white supremacy!" (Williams 1985).

Chapter 20   Williams's Psychosocial "Turning Point"

The psychosocial approach looks at individuals in the context of the combined influence that psychological factors and the surrounding social environment have on their physical and mental wellness and their ability to function.

The premise of Erikson's stages of psychosocial development is that a person's psychosocial development, from infant to elderly, depends on how certain psychosocial crises are resolved.

Erik Erikson (1902-1994) proposed that we all encounter certain crises that contribute to our psychosocial growth throughout our lifespan. He presented these crises as eight stages of psychosocial conflicts, often known as **Erik.**

Each of Erikson's psychosocial development stages is characterized by two contradictory emotional forces known as **contrary dispositions**, usually labeled as "syntonic" and "dystonic" dispositions. These dispositions cause a crisis or task that we need to resolve or master. When we resolve this crisis successfully, we acquire certain basic virtues and gain a sense of competence. Failure to do so may lead to feelings of inadequacy and a less healthy personality.

Erikson's Stages of Psychosocial Development

Approximate Age	Psychosocial Crisis/Task	Virtue Developed
Infant - 18 months	Trust vs Mistrust	Hope
18 months - 3 years	Autonomy vs Shame/Doubt	Will
3 - 5 years	Initiative vs Guilt	Purpose
5 -13 years	Industry vs Inferiority	Competency
13 -21 years	Identity vs Confusion	Fidelity
21- 39 years	Intimacy vs Isolation	Love
40 - 65 years	Generativity vs Stagnation	Care
65 and older	Integrity vs Despair	Wisdom

(C) The Psychology Notes Headquarters - https://www.PsychologyNotesHQ.com

Erikson Stages of Psychosocial Development in Plain Language

This phase of Erikson's stages of psychosocial development happens during adolescence(13-21 years old). This stage marks the shift from childhood to adulthood. It is also the turning point where "what the person has come to be" meets "the person society expects one to become."

At this stage, young people experience a lot of changes in their body. They begin to contemplate on the role they want to play in the adult world. They examine existential questions such as "Who am I?" and "What can I be?". At the young age of eleven, we see Robert Franklin Williams making a moral decision to be different from the adult black males who looked on helplessly at the beaten black woman he saw at the courthouse square in Monroe, North Carolina.

Young people, such as Robert Williams, who succeeded at this stage (the shift from childhood to adulthood—a turning point) developed a strong sense of identity. For example, when he came across challenges and problems, he committed to his principles, ideals and beliefs and his strong sense of what society should value=the dignity and rights of human beings to be protected by the laws of the Constitution. Those who fail to establish their own identity at this stage tend to be confused about themselves and about their future. They may end up following other people's ideas. We see that our hero, Robert Franklin Williams clearly moved to a decision "absent of confusion" **with defined sense of who he was!**

Erikson's theory of psychosocial development suggests that young people who succeed at resolving the crisis at this stage develops the virtue of "fidelity". This is characterized by the self-esteem and self-confidence that are requisite to associating freely with people and beliefs on the basis of their value, loyalty, and integrity. Other culturally-based developmental tasks include achieving gender-appropriate roles and becoming a responsible citizen.

Robert Franklin Williams' physiological maturations developed at an early age via the connectedness of two loving parents and his extended family members: grandparents and uncles who not only provided stability in his life, but further, carried on continuous discussions, readings, and family stories, in the home that helped him learn values and a strong sense of belongingness. His psychology (personal values and goals), as well as his sociology (specific culture to which the individual belongs), his cultural-based development and gender-appropriate role helped him make an important decision at an early age when he made the "all important" decision to be different, he stepped into the role of a responsible citizen, different from the helpless and powerless black men he encountered in Monroe at the impressionable age of eleven.

Chapter 21 Robert F. Williams in Cuba

A charismatic and powerful leader left an ineffaceable mark on the Monroe consciousness and the world. In my Interview with Robert Franklin Williams, his famous last words to me in 1985, he stated, "What I've witnessed is that this country kills our Black heroes for loving their country—Malcolm was killed, King was killed. I do not wish to die like that. This psychological disobedience would rise up, and I remember the 500 or so FBIs chasing me with their dogs as I escaped from Monroe into Canada to avoid Mauney, the Monroe police chief's **PROMISE to lynch me**. The image of the sled dog Husky and the Royal Canadian Mounted Police were always in my mind because of what they represented. The television newsreel of the dogs that showed before the actual featured film in the 60s; their motto was, 'We always get our man.' Unlike Malcolm and King, I don't want them to get me. I want to die at home in my bed" (Williams 1985).

Trumped-up charges forced Williams to leave the U.S. He was persecuted for advocating the use of armed self-defense against Klan violence in his hometown.

Robert Franklin Williams, his wife and two sons were forced to live in exile, first in Cuba and next in China following the phony kidnapping charge created by the Monroe chief of police accusing him of withholding, against their will, the white couple he sheltered from the angry mobs in his home for their own protection.

While living in Cuba for five years, during which time he wrote *Negroes with Guns* (1962), a title that was later used for a documentary (2005) on Williams and the Black Power movement.

In Cuba, Williams wrote, "…After we had left Monroe the US Justice Department, in collaboration with the chief of police, A.A. Mauney, released 250,000 "wanted" circulars and in these circulars, they described me as being schizophrenic. What happened in Monroe and continues to happen illustrates an old truth—that words used in common by all men do not always have a meaning common to all men. Men have engaged in life-or-death struggles because of differences of meaning in the commonly held words. The white racist believes in "freedom," he believes in "fair trial," he believes in "justice." He sincerely believes in these words and can use them with great emotion because to the white racist they mean his freedom to deprive Negroes of their basic human rights, and his courts where a "fair trial" is that procedure, and "justice" that decision which upholds the racists mad ideal of white supremacy…" (Williams was a pivotal influence on Huey P. Newton, founder of the Black Panther Party).

While in exile he began the anti-racist "Radio Havana Cuba" broadcast from Cuba. He established the station with approval of Cuban President Fidel Castro, along with assistance of the Cuban citizens, and operated it from 1962 to 1965. During the Cuban Missile Crisis in 1962, Williams used Radio Havana Cuba to urge black soldiers in the U.S. armed forces, who were then preparing for a possible invasion of Cuba, to engage in insurrection against the United States. **(WILLIAMS RESEARACH PAPERS).**

Cuba and Williams were not strangers. He had visited Havana the previous year, appearing on television and giving lectures throughout the country. With Williams back in Cuba, Havana's Union Radio announced that he "hoped to reach a great number of Negroes in the south of the United States through the powerful radio station 'Radio Havana Cuba.'

"Williams was always intent on getting his message out," explains Jon Elliston, author of "Psywar on Cuba." "Robert Williams Reports" became a regular part of Radio Havana's English program by 1962, but it was heard at first only on shortwave. Williams described what happened in oral history interviews with Robert Cohen and Thomas Mosby.

He wanted to be on AM with his own radio program, but faced opposition from American communists exiled in Cuba as well as elements of the Cuban government. He had listened to Cuba on the AM band when he was living in North Carolina; he knew AM was the way to reach an American audience. At first Cuban authorities tried to direct him to a weak AM station rather than the 50,000 watt one he wanted. Williams insisted and got his station.

He also faced opposition over programming, being urged to do a program for the white working class. He thought issues of blacks should be addressed first, and prevailed.

There was a battle over music next. Williams wanted to play the latest jazz. But this was "imperialist music" and he was urged to play Cuban opera instead. He explained that no one would listen to his words if they were accompanied by unpopular music.

The opposition in the Cuban government delayed him for three months; it apparently took the intervention of Fidel Castro to get Williams on AM with his desired programming.

Williams later called his program "Radio Free Dixie" and invited people to tune in every Friday night from 11 p.m. to midnight Eastern on 690 kHz for "jazz, Afro-American folklore, news, interviews and commentary" from "the free voice of the South." CMBC transmitted with 50,000 watts from Havana. Some American newspapers issued Williams' press release announcing the program. "The abundance of the USA belongs to the people, all the people, and no one faction has the right to deny the other liberty, justice and the pursuit of happiness," said Robert Williams in 1962.

He was speaking by way of the radio to listeners in the American South, but he was doing so from Cuba. (According to the documentary "Negroes With Guns): **The station** became the title of the book written about his life (Tyson1999).

In Cuba, he and Mabel aired an anti-racist radio show "Radio Free Dixie". **His radio show** was an African American, English-language radio program broadcast from Radio Havana from 1962 to 1965 that called upon "oppressed Negroes to rise and free themselves." Narrated by Robert Franklin Williams himself, the civil rights and political activist, the show was directed at southern blacks but was heard by listeners all over the United States and Canada. Additionally, Robert and Mabel continued to publish their newspaper, *The Crusader*, for thousands of subscribers.

For Blacks in the diaspora the revolutionary government of Cuba under the leadership of Fidel Castro has been and indispensable asset. Cuba has long been a place of refuge and support for persecuted Blacks in America. When State Troopers tried to murder and then falsely imprison Assata Shakur it was Cuba under Fidel Castro that offered her political asylum.

When the American Justice System tried to legally lynch the civil rights Leader Robert Franklin Williams — for promoting armed Black self-defense against the Ku Klux Klan and other white terrorist groups— it was Cuba that offered refuge. Fidel Castro himself was personally instrumental in helping Williams to setup Radio Free Dixie which broadcasted messages of freedom to Blacks in the Southern United States from Cuba.

During the Cuban Missile Crisis in 1962, Williams used Radio Free Dixie to urge Black soldiers in the U.S. armed forces, who were then preparing for a possible invasion of Cuba, to engage in insurrection against the United States.

Cubans In Florida

Fidel Castro once famously said that he was going to flush the toilets of Cuba on America, this "flush" eventually culminated in what became known as the Mariel boatlift, in which anyone who wanted to leave Cuba was allowed to leave and thousands did so by boat, he also emptied the prisons and mental asylums of Cuba and sent thousands of criminals to Miami which eventually led to what became known as the Cuban Crime Wave of the 1980's. This crime wave and the so-called "Marielito's" were immortalized in the film "Scarface".

As the political leader of Cuba until 2008, Fidel Castro was the first leader in the country to rule under Communism's policies. Although Fidel Castro had his shortcomings, when Black people were fighting for their lives and liberty in South Africa, Angola, Cape Verde, Guinea Bissau, Burkina Faso and the United States it was Fidel Castro and the people of Cuba who provided support and assistance.

****

Unfortunately, upon a later falling out with Castro in 1966, because of the reduced wattage of his Radio Free Dixie broadcast which had been minimized, and could only be transmitted to a small audience in the United States, Robert F. Williams made the decision to leave Cuba.

He and his wife Mabel in 1963 had visited China and Vietnam. However, before his stay in China, in the meanwhile, Robert Williams took up the lantern to bring attention to the "racist

American's slaughter of the people of color of Vietnam."

A plan was formulated under which North Vietnam invited Robert Williams to come and set up a newscast station to reach the Black American troops fighting in South Vietnam.

According to Williams, "While you are armed, remember this is your only chance to be free. ... This is your only chance to stop your people from being treated worse than dogs...

"Williams' cause against Black Americans fighting in Vietnam compares to famed boxing legend Muhammed Ali's refusal to honor the draft, Ali's, a man of strong principles, **refusal** to step forward in Houston in 1967 saw himself stripped of his boxing license and World Boxing Assigned title, and it stopped him from traveling abroad. Ali was convicted and given five years in prison for refusing induction into the United States draft as mandated by the Selective Service Act because in 1964 he was a part of the Nation of Islam and a

■■

converted Muslim. He refused to fight in Vietnam on the hardships he faced; **the** hypocrisy **of** America sending Black people, who were facing Jim Crow. Ali saw the war in Vietnam as an exercise in genocide. (1967 Ali/Draft Invasion).

Upon Williams' decision to leave Cuba, the civil rights leader in exile, in search for refuge, sent correspondences to many world leaders. Only Mao answered him.

Mao answered Robert Williams' request to live in China in 1962. Robert Franklin Williams and Mabel were invited to live as honored guests. He urged Mao-Tse-tung to issue his famous message of support to African Americans against the Viet Nam War (The Crusader):Ideas on the Vietnam War]

Chapter 22 Williams in China

Before Williams' transition, this era was at the height of the Cultural Revolution, and there was much political turmoil in China.

The Cultural Revolution included: by 1962 in many areas of rural China, indeed the collective system in agriculture had broken down completely, and individual farming was revived. Throughout 1961 and most of 1962, the central officials worked to consolidate their power and to restore faith in their leadership and goals.

Increasingly preoccupied with indoctrinating its heirs and heeding back to revolutionary days, Beijing's leaders closest in outlook to **Mao Zedong** and Lin Biao viewed the soldier-communist as the most suitable candidate for the second- and third-generation leadership. Army uniformity and discipline, it was seen, could transcend the divided classes, and all army men could be made to comply with the rigorous political standards set by Mao's leadership.

Upon Robert Franklin Williams first trip to the People's Republic of China in 1963, he and wife Mabel arranged for their two sons **John C. Williams, and Robert F. Williams, Jr.** to live and to study in China. (Franklin H. Williams the third son was born in later years).

When Williams elected to transition to China, he and his wife emigrated to China in 1966 at the personal invitation as a distinguished guest of Mao Zedong; in China they joined their two sons.

When Mao formally launched the Cultural Revolution in August 1966, he had already shut down the schools. He encouraged the Red Guards to attack all traditional values and "bourgeois" things and to put CCP (Communist Chinese Party) officials to the test by publicly criticizing them. These attacks were known at the time as struggles against the Four Olds (i.e., old ideas, customs, culture, and habits of mind), and the movement quickly escalated to committing outrages. intellectuals and many elderly people were physically abused, and many died. Mao nevertheless declared that it would be more beneficial than harmful to let the Cultural Revolution continue for several more months.

The Red Guards splintered into zealous factions, each purporting to be the "true" representative of the thought of Mao Zedong. Mao's own personal sect. Encouraged so as to provide momentum to the movement, assumed religious proportions. The resulting **anarchy**, terror, and paralysis threw the urban economy into a tailspin. Industrial production for 1968 dipped 12 percent below that of 1966.

While the forces **deployed** as of late 1968 were not adequate for a full-scale invasion of China, they certainly posed a serious menace, especially given the political division and social chaos that still prevailed in much of the country.

In China under Mao Zedong party recruitment procedures were tightened, and a major thought-reform movement was launched within the cadres' ranks. The Central Committee also established six supraprovincial regional bureaus charged with enforcing obedience to **Beijing** and bringing the new procedures for control into line with local conditions. The army, now firmly under **Lin Biao**, took the lead, beginning with a "purification" movement against dissidents within its own ranks.

Increasingly preoccupied with indoctrinating its heirs and harking back to revolutionary days, Beijing's leaders closest in outlook to **Mao Zedong** and Lin Biao viewed the soldier-communist as the most suitable candidate for the second- and third-generation leadership. Army uniformity and discipline, it was seen, could **transcend** the divided classes, and all army men could be made to comply with the rigorous political standards set by Mao's leadership.

In China Robert Williams became a friend and advisor to Mao Zedong.

Robert and wife Mabel visited communes and factories and spoke about the civil rights struggle in the United States. In China, he was at the seat of power, at Mao's side during many historic events. He spoke at length with Ho Chi Minh who described how Marcus Garvey had radicalized him in New York, where he worked as a busboy. He also described how the Vietnamese had dealt with Black US servicemen they had captured: they put them in separate camps and taught them African and Black American history. Many of these refused to go back to the US and are unknowingly celebrated by the black POW flag flown in front of many.

In a tour of Africa in late 1963 and early 1964, Zhou Enlai startled his hosts by calling for revolution in newly independent states and openly challenging the Soviet Union for the leadership of the Third World. Simultaneously, China challenged the U.S. system of alliances by establishing formal relations with France and challenged the Soviet Union's system by forming closer ties with Albania.

When the Soviet Union signed the **Nuclear Test-Ban Treaty** with the **United States** and **Great Britain** in **August 1963**, Chinese articles accused the Soviets of joining an anti-Chinese conspiracy. Confronted by this new strategic situation, the Chinese shifted their priorities to support an antiforeign line and promote the country's "self-reliance." Mao's calls for "revolutionization" acquired a more nationalistic aspect, and the PLA (People's Liberation Army) assumed an even larger place in Chinese political life.

This period of time has come to be interpreted as one of major decision within China. One ingredient of the debate was whether to prepare rapidly for conventional war against the United States or to continue the revolutionization of Chinese society, which in Mao's view had fundamental, long-term importance for China's security.

Initiated by Mao Zedong and Lin Biao, the purge first struck dissident army leaders, especially the chief of staff; as the power struggle began, China turned its back on the war in Vietnam and other external affairs.

It is unclear about Robert F. Williams thoughts (if any) about this dichotomy.

The September meeting may be taken as a clear representation of what came to be known as the Great Proletarian Cultural Revolution.

Beginning in 1963, Mao called on all Chinese to "learn from the PLA." Then, starting in 1964, Mao insisted that political departments modeled on those in the PLA be established in all major government bureaucracies.

In general, China during 1961–65 did a remarkable job of reviving the economy, at least regaining the level of output of 1957 in almost all sectors. Mao and a few of his supporters, however, still viewed class struggle and mass mobilization as core ingredients in keeping the revolutionary vision alive. Mao personally lost considerable prestige over the failure of the Great Leap—and the party's political and organizational apparatus was damaged—but he remained the most powerful individual in China.

Gradual transference of the revolution to top echelons of the party was managed by a group centered on Mao Zedong, Lin Biao, Jiang Qing, Kang Sheng, and Chen Boda. In May 1966 Mao secretly assigned major responsibilities to the army in cultural and educational affairs. Another purpose of the Cultural Revolution, as then conceived, would be a "revolution in the superstructure": a transformation from a bureaucratically run machine to a more popularly based system led personally by Mao and a simplified administration under his control.

A stifling of the revolutionary upsurge was supposedly evident in regulations of June 1964 for the organization of poor and lower-middle-peasant associations, and by early 1965 Mao could point to bureaucratic tendencies throughout the rural areas. In a famous document on problems arising in the course of the socialist education campaign, usually referred to as the "Twenty-three Articles," Mao in January 1965 stated for the first time that the principal enemy was to be found within the party, and he once more proclaimed the urgency of class struggle and mass-line politics.

While the forces deployed as of late 1968 were not adequate for a full-scale invasion of China, they certainly posed a serious menace, especially given the political division and social chaos that still prevailed in much of the country.

As the Cultural Revolution gained momentum, Mao turned for support to the youth as well as the army. In seeking to create a new system of education that would eliminate differences between town and country, workers and peasants, and mental and manual labor, Mao struck a responsive chord with the youth; it was their response that later provided him with his best shock troops. As a principal purpose, the Cultural Revolution was launched to revitalize revolutionary values for the successor generation of Chinese young people.

A second purpose of the Cultural Revolution would be the elimination of leading cadres Peng Zhen and Lu Dongyi and subsequently of Zhou Yang, then tsar of the arts and literature, indicated that this was to be a thoroughgoing purge whom Mao held responsible for past ideological sins and alleged errors in judgment.

The first speech by Robert F. Williams in China's Great Hall of the People was in 1968 on the third anniversary of Mao Zedong's speech against racial discrimination in the United States and in support of African Americans in their civil rights struggles. Topics include black power; history of African Americans; President Lyndon B. Johnson; Robert F. Kennedy; and Vietnam.

Over the next few years, Robert Franklin Williams traveled extensively throughout Asia and Africa, speaking out against racism, colonialism, and the war in Vietnam.

In 1968 while still in exile, but now living in Tanzania, Williams was named the first president of the Republic of New Africa.

In the meanwhile, he established-through radio, newsletters, and correspondence- a revolutionary black liberation front in the United States. During the Vietnam War, the activist-in-exile, Robert F. Williams met with Ho Chì Minh and made broadcasts to African-American soldiers on behalf of Hanoi and Beijing.

As a renowned leader in the African American armed self-defense movement, **Robert Franklin Williams** was thrilled to receive unprecedentedly strong support from **Mao** through their discussions, charting the depictions and functions of China in African American social movements for civil rights and Black Power. At that time, he readily became an enthusiastic promoter for an armed revolution in the United States. With sensitivity to the complexities and distinctions within the Chinese receptions to black nationalism, this was a dynamic, ever-evolving story that somewhat corresponded but did not absolutely connect with either political currents within China (such as the Cultural Revolution) or African American civil rights movement. Williams came to be aware that this dichotomy-- division or contrast between the two political causes as being opposed or entirely different. Although Mr. Williams was fighting for civil rights for Black Americans, he was also being used as an instrument by Cuba and China to weaken the global opinion of the US in their fight against communism. And, however; once Robert F. Williams decided to go back to the United States in late 1967, he gradually turned down the call for armed revolution and shifted his focus to challenging government law as well as racial discrimination through legal battles in courts (Ruodi 2016).

Back in the United States while Williams was in exile, in 1968 two brothers, Robert F. Milton Henry, also known as "Brother Gaidi Obadele," and Imari Abubakari Obadele organized a meeting of 500 black nationalists in Detroit, Michigan and founded The Republic of New Afrika (RNA), a black nationalist organization and black separatist movement popularized by black freedom fighter groups in the United States. Williams was named the international chairman of the Revolutionary Action Movement and elected as the first president-in-exile of the "Republic of New Africa." In this role, he traveled throughout the developing world.

The RNA group wrote a declaration of independence establishing the Republic of New Africa. The larger New Afrika movement in particular documented three main goals:

*Creation of an independent black-majority country situated in the Southeastern United States, in the heart of an area of black-majority population: South Carolina, Georgia, Alabama, Mississippi, and Louisiana.

*Payment by the federal government of several billion dollars in reparations to African-American descendants of slaves for the damages inflicted on Africans and their descendants by chattel enslavement, Jim Crow laws, and modern-day forms of racism.

*A referendum of all African Americans to determine their desires for citizenship; movement leaders say their ancestors were not offered a choice in this matter after emancipation in 1865 following the American Civil War.

*The RNA became a target for both local government and the FBI leading to the killing and injury of law-enforcement officials, raids and incarceration of its members due largely to alleged anti-radical program of surveillance, disruption and subversion. Members became convicted on federal conspiracy charges. Eleven RNA members including founder Imari Obadle were arrested and convicted for assault, murder and sedition. The RNA's popularity and influence diminished with most of its leaders in prison, but the membership of 5K to 10K still exist with headquarters in Washington, DC. Greve, E. (2012, March, 10).

When President Richard Nixon's administration launched secret contacts with China in the late 1960s, in 1970-71, Robert F. Williams bartered his knowledge of the Chinese government for safe passage home and a Ford Foundation grant to work at the Center for Chinese Studies at the University of Michigan. Drawing from his extensive stay in China, Williams advised political scientist Allen Whiting who in turn advised Henry Kissinger shortly before Kissinger's first trip to China. Due predominantly to his influence, China and the U.S broke the ice of a 20 year war of silence and began diplomatic relations. Robert Williams espoused armed self-defense when Huey Newton was still in high school. While the Nation of Islam talked about self-defense, The Black Guard was actually repelling Klan violence.

Under an official invitation from the Communist regime, many African-American activists, including W. E. B. Du Bois, Shirley Graham Du Bois, Robert F. Williams, Mabel Williams, Vicki Garvin, Huey Newton, and Elaine Brown, traveled to and even stayed for extended periods in the PRC over the next decade-and-a-half. As special guests carefully chosen by Beijing, they toured both the cities and the countryside, delivered speeches at mass rallies, and had their writings published in Chinese. Once back in the United States, they appeared on television and radio shows, gave public talks, and published articles in journals and newspapers, sharing their experiences in and thoughts about the PRC. With all traditional diplomatic, commercial, and cultural ties between the two countries terminated, the visits of these African-American activists not only allowed Beijing to maintain a controlled flow of people and information across the Pacific, but also provided it with a new instrument to engage and challenge Washington on the cultural front in the Cold War.

It is felt by some schools of thought that **Robert Williams' visits to China**, not only led to a transnational alliance that helped reinforce violent rebellions in both nations, but it is felt also that his exile in China exposed the black activist to the implosion caused by the Cultural Revolution in the Communist country.

Perhaps the stay in China may have caused Robert F. Williams to became more aware of his disagreement with the Chinese Communist leaders on **class struggle**. However, on the contrary, I'm not convinced that he became more appreciative of any progress made in civil rights struggle through peaceful reforms, and more confident in American political system based on the Constitution. It is evident that the Black man is ***still today*** struggling for peaceful reforms and representation of his equal rights within the political system of the nation's Constitution. Case in point: 21st century movements, i.e., Black Lives Matter demonstrators unfortunately have had to engage into forms of destruction in an endeavor to express deep rooted forms of rage from decades of brutality inflicted upon persons of color with impunity.

This memorandum of understanding (MOU) reaffirms the commitment to the development of a new model of U.S.-China military-to-military relations, which is an integral part of the bilateral relationship between the two nations.

Marking the failure of Beijing's effort to integrate the civil rights movement into the world revolution led by Mao, the transition of Robert Williams from an ardent promoter for armed revolution to a non-violence activist demonstrated the diversity and complexity of the U.S.-China relations in the 1960s. Consider what can be meant by the "global 1960s."

The U.S.-China relations of the 1960s will stage discussions on key ideas about the period 1960-69, such as Black Power and Third World issues, that transformed understandings of race, ethnicity, and power. **Hongshan, Li**.

Chapter 23 Robert and Mabel's Return to America

Robert Williams' wife Mabel Williams returned to the United States first. She entered the United States from Africa in September 1969.

When he was allowed to return to the United States, Robert Franklin Williams returned via London, England to Detroit, Michigan. While living in Michigan I reiterate, his intention was to fight extradition to North Carolina until the kidnapping charges were dropped. But no sooner than the plane transporting him touched down on American soil, he was immediately arrested for extradition to North Carolina. Williams surrendered and was freed on a $10,000 bond after a fiery courtroom scene where he described himself as "the victim in this case" for trial in Monroe on the kidnapping charge. According to a Charlotte Observer article staff writer, during the trial, Williams' anger flared when Judge John McConnell tried imposing a $20,000 bond. Williams rose and asked McConnell if he could make a statement, he pointed out, "Since I am the victim in this case." He went on to say, "It's white supremacy, that's what it is." Williams replied also, that he would prefer going to jail to posting what he considered an unjust bond. He conveyed to the judge, "You know deep down in your heart this is a frame-up." He continued, "This is the worst form of American justice."

Williams was tried in Monroe, North Carolina in December 1975. The historian Gwendolyn Midlo Hall chaired his defense committee and a broad range of leftists arrived in town. (In the 19th and 20th centuries and since then, the term *left-wing* has been applied to a broad range of movements including civil rights movements, anti- war movements and environmental movements, as well as a wide range of parties). arrived in town.

Attorney William Kunstler represented Williams in court. The state of North Carolina dropped all phony kidnaping, extradition; wanted armed and dangerous, charges against Robert F. Williams almost immediately.

When Robert Williams returned to the United States, it was done with his withdrawal from leadership and the discreet prearrangement of the current President Richard Nixon,(1969-74) as a "Gesture Of Goodwill" in the president's efforts to cultivate the Chinese leadership for his historic visit to China. Mr. Nixon's objective was to analyze what Robert Williams knew about China and his relationship with Mao. In February 1972, Nixon and his wife traveled to China. Kissinger briefed Nixon for over 40 hours in preparation. Upon touching down, the President and First Lady emerged from Air Force One and greeted Chinese Premier Zhou Enlai. Nixon made a point of shaking Zhou's hand, something which then-Secretary of State John Foster Dulles had refused to do in 1954 when the two met in Geneva. More than a hundred television journalists accompanied the president. On Nixon's orders, television was strongly favored over printed publications, as Nixon felt that the medium would capture the visit much better than print. It also gave him the opportunity to snub the print journalists he despised.

Nixon and Kissinger met for an hour with Mao (Mao Zedong, also known as Chairman Mao, was a Chinese communist revolutionary who became the founding father of the People's Republic of China (PRC), which he ruled as the chairman of the Communist Party of China from its establishment in 1949 until his death in 1976), and Zhou (The Zhou dynasty lasted longer than any other dynasty in Chinese history) at Mao's official private residence, where they discussed a range of issues. Mao later told his doctor that he had been impressed by Nixon, whom he considered forthright, unlike the leftists and the Soviets. He said he was suspicious of Kissinger, though the National Security Advisor referred to their meeting as his "encounter with history". A formal banquet welcoming the presidential party was given that evening in the Great Hall of the People. The following day, Nixon met with Zhou; the joint communique following this meeting recognized Taiwan as a part of China, and looked forward to a peaceful solution to the problem of reunification. When not in meetings, Nixon toured architectural wonders including the Forbidden City, Ming Tombs, and the Great Wall.

With this collaboration with President Richard Nixon, Robert Franklin Williams, who had previously walked the soil in Beijing, China, had been instrumental in Americans receiving their first glimpse into Chinese life through the cameras which accompanied Pat Nixon, who toured the city of Beijing and visited communes, schools, factories, and hospitals.

The visit ushered in a new era of Sino-American relations, (Chinese–U.S. relations, or Sino-American relations, refers to relations between China and the United States since the 18th century). Fearing the possibility of a Sino-American alliance, the Soviet Union yielded to pressure for cooperation with the United States.

Even though the FBI had warned Nixon that Williams could likely fill the role of assassinated Civil Rights Leaders such as that of Malcolm X and Martin Luther King, but after assessing the state of The Movement In 1970, prevalent with irritating Internal philosophical divisions, murders and incarceration of numerous black militants, Williams, now disheartened, he withdrew from all but nominal leadership in the militant groups that were founded in his name. The material on his disillusionment with "The Movements" for example: founder of the *Revolutionary Action Movement; Forefather of Black Power Movement;* Williams' open advocacy of armed self-defense anticipated the movement for " black power " in the late 1960s and helped inspire groups like the Student National Coordinating Committee, the Revolutionary Action Movement, and the Black Panther Party. Robert Williams also championed the Cuban Revolution. He had saved lives in a 1959 race riot and took on the defense of two youths (aged 7 and 9) accused of "assaulting and molesting a white female] He had fought against Scapegoat Psychology: miscarriage of justices.

Robert Franklin Williams is a subject of vast research significance in and of itself.

Robert Williams in Monroe following his return to North Carolina from China. Pictured with his brother Jon Williams, left. Williams' Family Reunion post.

Shortly after he returned, the approaching period of truce augured a warming of relations with the People's Republic of China.

Briefly: From the 1960s onwards, nations friendly to the PRC, led by the **People's Republic of Albania under Enver Hoxha**, moved an annual resolution in the General Assembly to expel the "representatives of Chiang Kai-shek" (an implicit reference to the ROC) and permit the PRC to represent China at the UN. Every year the United States was able to assemble enough votes to block this resolution. Both sides rejected compromise proposals to allow both states to participate in the UN, based on **the One-China policy.**[The admission of newly independent developing nations in the 1960s gradually turned the General Assembly from being Western-dominated to being dominated by countries sympathetic to the PRC. Not only the newly founded developing countries, but also most of the Western countries eventually decided to recognize the PRC. During the 1950s and 1960s, United Kingdom, **Switzerland, Sweden**, and France shifted their recognition of China from the ROC (Republic of China) to the PRC (People's Republic of China). In the early 1970s, **Canada, Turkey**, and more western countries established diplomatic relations with the PRC, and severed diplomatic relations with the ROC. (See more from): Republic of China in the United Nations (1945–1971).

****

As a tired man, Robert F. Williams settled in Baldwin Michigan and lectured at The University of Michigan while writing his memoirs: *While God Lay Sleeping,* until the kidnapping charges were dropped in 1975.

During his exile and after his return to the U.S., he continued to fight racism. He and his wife, Mabel, published the militant journal *Crusader* and broadcast a radio program called *Radio Free Dixie*.

At this point, I'm not ready for our hero, Robert Franklin to expire just yet.

Malcolm X spoke fondly of the civil rights activists Robert Franklin Williams; always referring to him as a forerunner in the movement of self-defense. Realizing that the two of them were supporters of the same cause, civil rights and reliance on one's own power and resources.

Chapter 24 Scapegoat Justice in the South: How it Works

The kind of justice Robert Franklin Williams continued to put his life on the line for: his audacity to bring attention to as stated by Circuit Court Judge Carmen Mullen after two black youths ages 14 and 21 were executed for a crime they did not commit. "I can think of no greater injustice than the violation of one's Constitutional rights which has been proven to me in this case."

A miscarriage of justice took place in Alcolu, SC in March of 1944. A 14-year-old boy, George Stinney, Jr. was arrested, after two young white girls were discovered brutally murdered in a watery ditch. At the time of George's arrest, he was home with his older brother and younger sister. George and his older brother Johnnie were arrested and taken away, even though their parents weren't home. George and his little sister were reported to be the last people to see the girls alive. According to George's sister, Amie Ruffner, "[The police] were looking for someone to blame it on, so they used my brother as a scapegoat."

On June 16, 1944, George Stinney was executed! He became the youngest person in modern times to be put to death.

After 70 years, Mr. Stinney was exonerated of the double murders. This horrendous moment from the Jim Crow South has tormented civil rights advocates for years.

On the day of his arrest, George was interrogated in a small room by himself, without his parents or an attorney present. The police alleged that George confessed to the killings because he wanted to have sex with one of the girls.

A copy of a photo that ran June 8, 1944, in The Columba (S.C.) Record, showing Stinney, center right, and Bruce Hamilton, 21, center left, enter the death house in the state prison. Both were executed June 16, 1944.

George Stinney was rushed to trial. With his trial taking only two hours to complete, and a jury deliberating for just 10-minutes, George was convicted of murder on April 24, 1944. He was sentenced to die by electrocution and at the time, 14 was the age of criminal responsibility. Mr. Stinney was represented by a lawyer who was a

local political figure and the lawyer made the decision not to appeal the conviction.

There was practically no evidence presented and it showed how a young black child was railroaded by an all-white justice system.

Up to the point where he was recently exonerated, no written record of a confession was ever found. With new facts in the case coming to light, Circuit Judge Carmen Mullen vacated George's conviction; 70 years after he was executed. The judge remarked, "I can think of no greater injustice than the violation of one's Constitutional rights which has been proven to me in this case." A former cellmate of George's at the time, issued a statement saying the boy denied the charges. "I didn't, didn't do it,' " Wilford Hunter said Stinney told him. "He said, 'Why would they kill me for something I didn't do?" The case has haunted the town of Alcolu since 1944.

The Stinney family claimed that George's confession was coerced and that he had an alibi, his sister. His sister said she was with him at the alleged time of the crime. They were watching their family's cow graze near the railroad tracks by their house when the two girls rode over on their bicycles and asked them a question. George was accused of murdering the girls as they picked wildflowers.

According to George's brother, Charles, the Stinney family fled their home because "George's conviction and execution was something my family believed could happen to any of us in the family. Therefore, we made a decision for the safety of the family to leave it be," Charles Stinney wrote in his sworn statement.

Demands for a new trial were made by the Stinney family. Judge Mullen heard sworn testimony from George's brothers and sisters, a witness from the search party that discovered the bodies and experts who challenged his confession. A child psychiatrist testified that George's confession should have never been trusted. The psychiatrist, Amanda Sales, stated that, "It is my professional opinion, to a reasonable degree of medical certainty, that the confession given by George Stinney Jr. on or about March 24, 1944, is best characterized as a coerced, compliant, false confession. It is not reliable." George Stinney was sent to the electric chair a mere 84 days after the girls' deaths! Both were executed June 16, 1944.

Today, a death sentence is almost automatically appealed and it could take years, even decades, before an execution. In which time, new evidence could be discovered as in the case of George Stinney, he wasn't even 5 feet tall and weighed less than 100 pounds.

The straps on the electric chair couldn't contain his frail body. It was reported that George had to sit on books to reach the headpiece of the electric chair. The Stinney family maintained that they never wanted a pardon because "a pardon is forgiving someone for something they did," said Norma Robinson, George Stinney's niece. "That wasn't an option for my mother, my aunt or my uncle. We weren't asking forgiveness."

They wanted and received a full exoneration of the George Stinney, Jr. name. (Price 1944).

Chapter 25 Compilation of Photographs

Robert Franklin Williams: Williams Family Reunion Compilation of photographs.

Robert Franklin Williams

Robert Franklin Williams and wife Mabel Williams: Williams Family Reunion

Robert Williams and wife Mabel in Tanzania, Africa before living in China.

Song of the Exile
Sad is the distant voice calling
From my native and where Autumn is falling
My heart has a ceaseless yearning
For fellowship where kinsmen sit with home fires burning.
Oh, how I wish I were again a child
That I might hear my mother sing and see her blithely smile
Oh, how I long to see the old home place

More beautiful now with a touch of Autumn in her face.
Oh, to hear the hills and valleys serenaded by the wind
Would be a bit like heaven, if I were home again.
To hear the call of the wild geese winging overhead
A melancholy farewell to a little boy in bed.
Each night in dreams I stand at father's door
A prodigal son who is home once more
Each breath is a year, a heartbeat a mile
To the soul that sings of exile.
  --Robert F. Williams, October 11, 1966 Beijing

Robert F. Williams holding a copy of the *Crusader*

Photo of Robert Franklin Williams in China with Mao Zedong, researched papers.

The Cultural Revolution, formally the Great Proletarian Cultural Revolution, was a sociopolitical movement in China from 1966 until 1976. Launched by Mao Zedong, Chairman of the Communist Party of China (CPC), its stated goal was to preserve Chinese Communism by purging remnants of capitalist and traditional elements from Chinese society, and to re-impose Mao

Zedong Thought (known outside China as Maoism) as the dominant ideology in the CPC.

In China: Robert Franklin Williams (second from left) and his wife Mabel, (left) marched with Chinese officials in Peking at the 1967 celebration of International Labor Day.

Williams and his wife lived in China for three years. Imagine being Robert Williams from the US western world walking the streets of Beijing at the height of the Chinese Cultural Revolution. He moved to China with his wife Mabel at the invitation of Mao Zedong, 1966.

Below: A letter written to me from Robert Franklin Williams, 1989, after I had returned to North Carolina and began a teaching career in Union County.

```
                                        P. O. Box 611
                                        Baldwin, Michigan 49304
                                        February 9, 1989

Mrs. Connie W. Sparks
6135 Meadow Rose Lane
Charlotte, North Carolina 28215

Dear Connie:
          Your letter was received and it was good to hear from you.
It was especially good to know that you are sensitive enough
to understand and see through the game being re-run on our
people. It is vital that our people speak out against racism
now. It is a grave error for us to think that racism has been
abolished. History repeats itself. After the Civil War and
during Reconstruction, Jim Crow and some phases of segregation
were partially abolished, however, it shortly reappeared. We
are witnessing a similar situation today.
          All across the nation a sometimes subtle and sometimes
violent racism is again casting its ugly shadow over American
society. Those who claim that we are "Free at last" or that
they do not harbor racial feelings are either naive, insensi-
tive or downright deceptive. It is indeed tragic that some
people are racists without being conscious of it. This is
because American society is so permeated with it that some
certain prejudice is considered normal. Yes, there has been
improvement for our people, but an improvement of an injustice
is not enough. There is no such thing as partial justice. In
order for justice to be real, it must be complete. Those who
have been conditioned from birth in this society and proclaim
themselves to be free of prejudice are deluding themselves.
The home is not the only place that spawns racism. It grows
from all facets of life whether visually or physically. It
is a learned trait that we are not necessarily conscious of.
          The deterioration of the African American family and
community is a reaction to racial oppression. One is conditioned
```

Connie - 2

by his environment. I noticed a statement in the article that you sent which inferred that Monroe's violence was due to Robert Williams. The statement overlooked the violence and degradation of the oppression we experienced. The American revolutionaries violently resisted their oppressors but they were not blamed for the violence. Only the prejudiced would blame the oppressed rather than the cruel oppressor. It means that such a person identifies with the side of the oppressor.

I resisted white racism because it was painful. It was thrust upon me by brutal white supremacists and I make no apologies for violently resisting. Racism is not abolished. Yes, and it was and is still in New York and the entire nation.

Sincerely,

Robert F. Williams

This letter is in response to a newspaper article I sent to Robert Franklin Williams given to me from a colleague at Piedmont High School, Mr. Tom Blansett. Ironically, the Newspaper article referenced Robert Williams as starting violence for defending himself against the most brutal incidents inflected by whites in Monroe, NC and for requesting that Constitutional laws be enforced to protect all citizens.

To celebrate Williams's return, Black Panther leader Huey P. Newton, as quoted in The Black Panthers Speak, wrote, " Greetings to the Republic of New Africa and President Robert Williams. I am very happy to welcome you back home. I must add that it is perfect timing. And we need you very much, the people need you very much".

After Returning to the United States Williams was given a grant by the Ford Foundation to work at the University of Michigan Center for Chinese Studies. He wrote *While God Lay Sleeping*: The Autobiography of Robert F. Williams.

While a research associate at The Institute For Chinese Studies, he and Mabel moved to the remote, historically integrated, Michigan township of Baldwin, where they remained for the rest of his life. In Baldwin, the Williams continued their dedication to social transformation, focusing on the local level. His role as a national leader subsided, but his image among the succeeding generation of black power advocates remains profound. Like the black folk Hero "John Henry," Robert F. Williams outwitted and tormented the oppressors of African Americans (Cameron Blogpost 2014).

****

After the return, Robert Williams and his wife, Mabel, continued to fight against racism and published the militant journal *Crusader* and broadcast a radio program called *Radio Free Dixie*.

In his battle against Hodgkin's disease, Williams was as brave as he had ever been. His memoirs, *While God Lay Sleeping: The Autobiography of Robert F. Williams*, tell the compelling story of a man who risked his life for democracy and a humanitarian vision that was rooted in the finest traditions of African-American striving. Above the desk where he wrote hung the ancient rifle that was a gift from his grandmother.

Robert Franklin Williams, my cousin on my grandfather Reverend Daniel Arthur Williams' side of the family, civil rights activist and president of the NAACP in Monroe, North Carolina in the 60s had a keen nose for storytelling. As Rosa Parks spoke of him at his 1996 eulogy.

Living out his final quest, to be called home while lying in the quiet of his own home in his own bed, unlike Martin Luther King Jr. and Malcolm X, the Civil Rights activists who had been murdered, Robert Franklin Williams, our hero, the heroic legend, died October 15, 1996, with his wife Mabel at his side in Grand Rapids, Michigan at age 7l from Hodgkin disease. Civil rights leader; former president of the NAACP Monroe, NC chapter, and author of the 1965 Manifesto, *Negroes With Guns*; Forefather of the movements of the 50s and 60s era; his story is a remarkable chapter in the history of Black liberation and human rights.

I was well into adulthood in 1996 when RW (Robert Franklin Williams, Sr.) was eulogized in my hometown, his birthplace in Monroe, NC. It was said by Mrs. Rosa Parks, the civil rights advocate, who's snapshot reflects her refusal in 1956 to give up her seat to a white man on the Montgomery bus, spoke so eloquently at his memorial, which I, along with hundreds of his family members and worldly figures attended. Ms. Parks proclaimed, "Those who marched with Martin Luther King Jr. in Alabama admired Mr. Williams for his courage and his commitment to freedom." She further declared, "Mr. Williams could have been a rich and famous man, but he chose to dedicate his life to the 'good fight' for justice and equality for his oppressed brothers and sisters.

Robert Franklin Williams was buried in a gray suit given by Mao Zedong; his casket was draped with a red, black, and green Pan African flag.

Ms. Rosa Parks described Robert Franklin Williams as, "A heroic black leader who had escaped the assassin's bullet and lived a long life. His name should go down in history and never be forgotten!"

Photograph: Rosa Parks far left with Connie Williams right, 1996, taken at the memorial for Robert Franklin Williams at Central United Methodist Church, Haynes St. in our (RFW and my) hometown Monroe, North Carolina.

Chapter 26 Commentaries About and by Robert F. Williams

This book represents much of what I stand for and believe in—in God, family, research, patience, goals, and a strive for some element of excellence, completion and some success. In 1984 when the idea to write this biography was conceived, I had met my cousin Robert Franklin Williams in person at the Holiday Inn Express Hotel in Monroe at one of our Williams' Family Reunion.

At that reunion he spoke directly to me about his feelings to leave Monroe going into exile and how he wanted to live not die like Malcolm and Dr. King. How our country kills our Black men because they love their country and freedom. He said, "Kennedy loved this country, he went on to become president." But we all know Kennedy was assassinated. Williams further stated, "I did not want to die like Malcolm and King, I wanted to die at home in my bed."

In writing my cousin Robert Franklin Williams' biography, it was important to be sensitive to what I knew about his life, his experiences and what he stood for relating to family, love of humanity and his honesty about the love he held in his heart for this country and particularly his own life.

Just as significant, I wanted to stay authentic to the unfolding of the history because of the momentous time period and what Mr. Williams had to endure growing up and living as an African American during the 50s and 60s in the South governed by strict Jim Crow law, when a Black child, woman and man could be *hanged* for the slightest infraction at the hands of racists supremist who disguised their true identity underneath a white sheet pulled over the head)— a time in history when the police, city council and authoritative figures protected a "scapegoat" group such as the Ku Klux Klan, allowing them to run rampantly through Monroe, NC and cities like Monroe, terrorizing and killing African Americans with impunity, and celebrating their cross burning tactics and destruction of property. When an African American could be killed for fighting back and were told to "turn the other cheek, examples of non-violent passive resistance, all while losing one's life.

In writing Robert Franklin Williams' story there were many times I came away from the written page with a lump in my throat and a paining heart because this "man" who was acting like a "MAN", standing up like a "man" unlike some sniveling coward that the "pink" man would prefer! From here on, I shall refer to Caucasian persons as pink. I do so, in all honesty, I have never experienced the sight of a so-called white person. Clouds are white, cotton is white, snow is white; therefore, I don't recall ever experiencing the visualization of a human the color of clouds, cotton or snow. *Yet persons continued to respond to the concept of white—a term pink people refer to themselves because it seems to allow them to perpetuate some false preeminence of superiority by referring to self as the color of clouds, cotton and snow.* Connie Williams 7-18-21.

I can compare this usage of certain concepts: the importance of certain words according to Robert Franklin Williams, who quotes, "words and their meanings are different and do not have the same meaning to the "white" man as the meaning to the African American (Black) man. In Cuba, Williams wrote, "...After we had left Monroe the US Justice Department, in collaboration with the chief of police, A.A. Mauney, released 250,000 "wanted" circulars and in these circulars, they described me as being schizophrenic. What happened in Monroe and continues to happen illustrates an old truth: that words used in common by all men do not always have a meaning common to all men. Men have engaged in life-or-death struggles because of differences of meaning in the commonly held words. The white racist believes in "freedom," he believes in "fair trial," he believes in "justice." He sincerely believes in these words and can use them with great emotion because to the white racist they mean his freedom to deprive Negroes of their basic human rights, and his courts where a "fair trial" is that procedure, and "justice" that decision which upholds the racists mad ideal of white supremacy…"

My philosophy regarding pigmentation is: The sooner we as a country of people begin to admit we are all people of color, the sooner our relationship with each other will improve and perhaps begin to heal itself so we may move on pass the extreme prejudices that exist.

In my research, I find that the oldest bones discovered belonged to a person of color which reveal generations of human derivatives from persons of color. Of all the skeletons on a list of ten skeletal remains, all were classified as having been identified from Native American or African heritage belonging to non-Caucasian remains.

The oldest skeletons are controversial because they were initially identified as being of

African heritage. Despite not being able to properly classify the Grimaldi Man skeletons, they have been claimed by the Afrocentrism movement as being black. (Oldest.Org)

Robert Franklin Williams wrote in *Negroes With Guns*, "The violence that we had in the 60's was limited. The next time it will be unlimited because the violence in the 60's was a struggle for human dignity and for human rights." In other words, the right to participate in the economics of our society without being held down because of the color of skin. Williams said, "The next struggle will be a struggle for survival and it will not just be limited to Black people or Black against white, but it will be the poor people, the masses of the people of the country, struggling for the right to live or the right to survive" (Williams, Robert Franklin Quotes).

If the concern is one of survival, it would appear that we would better benefit by learning cooperation, identification, association, bonding, empathy, a coming together as one—meaning we're all "people of color" with like hopes, desires, dreams for our fellow man/woman/children.

In writing Robert Franklin Williams biography, I experienced researching and writing one of the most challenging narratives of a lifetime to date. For one rationale is there is a vast wealth of literature available and documented about his remarkable life. I experienced this incredible honor and owe all of the power, honor and glory to my Almighty God for His favor, miracles and immortality bestowed upon my psyche and creative ability to decipher this written work.

I write this biography with hope that readers are decoding and comprehending with ethos. I welcome, the listeners. In the words of John Lewis, who said, **"Get in good trouble**, necessary trouble, and redeem the soul of America." **John Lewis** made this statement on the Edmund Pettus Bridge in Selma, Alabama on March 1, 2020 commemorating the tragic events of Bloody Sunday. Bloody Sunday occurred on March 7, 1965 as peaceful protesters were beaten by law enforcement officers for crossing the bridge. *Five-things-John-Lewis -taught-us*: (2020).

When I shared with my brother "Mac" (child # eight of twelve) Jones McConnie Williams Jr. the research I had completed for the presentation to be given at the "Lynching, Without Sanctuary" housed at The University of North Carolina, Center City Campus, and Levine Museum of the New South, at Charlotte, he, after perusing my findings, the writings I had completed, (those who read over my manuscript and research materials had to sign a list for verification). After signing his name, my brilliant brother wrote a note alongside his signature that specified, "Long Overdue."

I can immensely appreciate his comment. As I continue this endeavor, I feel this phase of the completed work is coming to a conclusion, but I do not feel it will ever be totally finished. The more I learn about my cousin, our legendary hero Robert Franklin Williams, "the man who miraculously escaped the hanging rope" –the man who extraordinarily escaped the hanging rope; the master-mind who escaped the hanging rope; the man who stumped the Ku Klux Klan and escaped the hanging rope in Monroe, North Carolina at a time when racists "pink" men put into practice every scapegoat maneuver known to man to take his precious life. The more I learn about him, the more I want to know, and desire for others to learn about him. The more I learn about him, the more empathy I have for him and what I truly believe was in his soul for his fellow man—and all citizens.

When I look at our dear cousin's photograph, I cannot help but feel—if only he could have been respected for his hard work—his dedication to the struggle/the cause for human decency protected by our Constitution.

In writing the story about a hero such as Robert Franklin Williams, I found it's almost impossible to contrive something that had not already been said and run the risk of leaving out any important event except for my very own researched exploration of the Lawrence Kohlberg analysis to Robert Franklin Williams' rationale for his decision making determination to "stand up" and fight against human helplessness a demand for inalienable human rights given by God. But isn't that the true mark of a hero—a legendary hero that his story continually gets told to generations yet to come? It's been a great honor to once more bring life and light into the story of our legendary hero, my beloved cousin Robert Franklin Williams.

When my dentist, Dr. Jeffery Phillippi read *Green* and the included EPILOGUE that chronology of events dramatizing the civil rights upheaval in Monroe in the early 60s, he confessed, " I looked up and read everything I could about Robert Franklin Williams. He was quite a guy."

I proudly write some of the accounts of his life and appropriately title his story *"Audacity Story of a Legendary Hero"* because without a doubt our cousin (the Williams' kinfolk attest to the facts), the late Robert Franklin Williams was and still is a legendary hero.

At a time in history when local blacks where in constant fear of powerful pink bigotry—the police department, the KKK and the horrors and indignities of Jim Crow law, **Williams took drastic**

measures to prevent possible lynching: Williams brought national attention to the incident of the famous "Kissing Case" involving two young black boys who may have been lynched; his heroic positioning the end of a double-barrel shotgun in the chest of a lynching mobster who came to fear he too might "bite the dust;" and finally, his own escape into exile with his wife and young children to prevent his own middle of the night lynching. Williams' ideology manifested as he fought against the brutality especially against black women (sparked by an incident he witnessed first-hand as a youth, the beating of a black woman as many looked on); further, the black church offered no noteworthy support nor improved pink community regard for laws when it came to race relations. Williams soon learned from experience that respect sometimes **only** came via shaming the nation with his storytelling of exigencies.

Williams' fight for social justice was marked by his relentless determination to bring safety for young black boys and girls who continued to lose their precious lives in the unsafe, murky water swimming holes during the 60s summer when their pink counterparts enjoyed the "pink only" tax-payers swimming pool at The Monroe Country Club. When pink men, alarmed that their children might have to share water with blacks of course a lynch-mob mentality emerged. And his story began and continued to unfold!

****

Robert Franklin Williams was answering a higher calling from God against what was illegal, immoral and unconstitutional, he was following an inner conviction espoused by his parents and the teachings of the Bible that should be respected and should be honored.

Monroe's Black Armed Guard wasn't a subsidiary of the Communist Party, nor an independent organization like the Black Panther Party that would use similar tactics of arming their members later. In fact, "Black Armed Guard" was nothing more than a fancy name for an officially chartered National Rifle Association chapter.

Eric Garner was choked to death when the police ignored the "poor man's plea" to allow him to breathe. He said, "I can't breathe; I can't breathe."

But the police officers chocked Eric Gainer to death because he was illegally selling cigarettes on the street. And now the officers are still walking around as free men—a twenty-first century lynching—a case of "Scapegoat lynching; an example of abuse of power directed against the black man where a black teenager pulled over in a pink neighborhood can lose his life.

His 1962 book, *Negroes With Guns* was visionary for the Black Power movement to come later on in the decade. But Williams is noteworthy for his lack of revolutionary zeal, at least predominantly. Williams was cautious to always uphold that the Black Armed Guard was not a treacherous organization, but one dedicated to providing defense to a group of people who were under attack and lacking in normal Constitutional legal remedies:

"To us there was no Constitution, no such thing as 'moral persuasion' – the only thing left was the bullet...I advocated violent self-defense because I don't really think you can have a defense against violent racists and against terrorists unless you are prepared to meet violence with violence, and my policy was to meet violence with violence." - Robert Williams.

"The price of freedom is eternal vigilance." - Thomas Jefferson

Shift Toward Militancy

In the late 1960s, disillusionment and bitterness grew among African Americans. Many young blacks especially had become dissatisfied with the nonviolent approach to achieving fairness and justice. King's murder reinforced their conviction that pinks were their enemies and could not be trusted. Although federal court decisions and laws were ending legal segregation, they could not remove the discrimination and prejudice that existed in the hearts and minds of many pinks.

Millions of people mourned the deaths by assassination of President John F. Kennedy in November 1963 and United States senator Robert F. Kennedy in June 1968. Both men were sympathetic to the struggle for equality.

I reiterate Robert Franklin Williams' words spoken to me in an interview of 2 July, 1984. At the Holiday Inn, Monroe, NC, where he was staying during the Williams' Family Reunion, he declared, "Our Black men are killed for loving their country. John F. Kennedy loved his country; yet, he became president; however, his struggle for equality helped precipitate his murder. He was killed before Malcolm X and Martin Luther King Jr. I didn't want to be killed like Kennedy, Malcolm X and Martin for loving freedom, and for trying to ensure that the Constitution applied to everyone." Williams, R.F. (personal communication), 1984.

A severe blow hit the Civil Rights movement when Dr. Martin Luther King Jr. was killed in Memphis, Tennessee, in April 1968. James Earl Ray, a racist high school dropout and prison escapee, pled guilty to the shooting and spent the rest of his life incarcerated. (The NC Museum of History).

Negroes With Guns

According to a provocative quote made by Robert Franklin Williams, included in the Prologue of his book, "I have asserted the right of Negroes to meet the violence of the Ku Klux Klan by armed self-defense—and have acted on it." Furthermore, he stated, "It has always been an accepted right of Americans." He also noted, "The history of our Western states proves, that where the law is unable, or unwilling, to enforce order, the citizens can, and must act in self-defense against lawless violence. I believe these rights hold true for black Americans as well as white Americans." (cited from *Negroes With Guns*: 2013).

Negroes With Guns

"Radio Free Dixie" was the title of Robert Franklin Williams' radio show in Cuba and later becomes the title of Dr. Tim Tyson's book: (1999).

American civil rights leader known for taking a militant stance against racism decades before the Black Power and black nationalist movements of the late 1960s and early '70s adopted similar philosophies. As early as the late 1940s, when the Federal Bureau of Investigation (FBI) began investigating him, Robert Franklin Williams was advocating armed self-reliance for migrant laborers and victims of civil rights abuses—views that were uncommon at the time among civil rights activists.

Robert F. Williams is considered by many to be the architect behind the modern Black Power movement. He was a highly influential figure for leaders of the Black Panthers and similar groups.

Williams famously wrote a 1962 manifesto that called for Black people to arm and defend themselves against racist pink oppressors. The Philosophy Of Robert F. Williams provided the intellectual foundation for America's most militant advocates of racial and social justice. From his actions, speeches, and writings emerged the foundation for The Black Power Movement. studying about Robert F. Williams is essential for all RBG (This definition appears rarely and is found in the following Acronym Finder categories: Organizations, NGOs, schools, universities, etc. Slang/chat, popular culture), learners who intends to draw lessons from the 1960's liberation struggle. His works will inform us on The Civil Rights And Black Power Movements, and American Radicalism, and on one of the most extraordinary political careers in American history.

If one could ask the leaders commonly associated with the Black Power and Black Nationalist Movements of the 1960s-Malcolm X, Kwame Torie (Stokely Carmichael), Jamail Al-amin (rap Brown), Amiri Baraka (LeRoi Jones), and Black Panthers Huey Newton, Bobby Seale and Eldridge Cleaver—what Individual had the greatest influence on their political development, surely one of the first to be named would be Robert Franklin Williams (Apr 01, 2016).

Robert Franklin Williams and African diaspora: the end of **slavery** and the decline of **colonialism**

Afrocentrism has its origins in the **work of African and African diaspora** intellectuals in the late 19th and early 20th centuries, following social changes in the United States and Africa due both to the end of slavery and the decline of colonialism.

Indeed, **Black intellectuals** during the period and since used a wide variety of cultural productions, and artistic works as a form of language artfully interweaving theatrical, musical, and ritual performance as a rich continuum of cultural exchange that imaginatively reinvented, re-created, and restored the centrality of African diaspora in the making of the modern Black Atlantic world.

On the surface, the term "Africana" refers to the African diaspora, that is, those who have ancestors from the African continent, though they may live elsewhere in the world; this includes primarily, though not exclusively, those identified as **African**, **Afro-Caribbean**, and **African-American]**

Diaspora refers simultaneously to a process, a condition, a space, and a discourse: the continuous processes by which a diaspora is made, unmade, and remade; the changing conditions in which it lives and expresses itself; the places where it is molded and imagined; and the contentious ways in which it is studied and discussed. In short, diaspora is a state of being and a process of becoming, a condition and consciousness located in the shifting interstices of "here" and "there," a voyage of negotiation between multiple spatial and social identities. Created out of movement—dispersal from a homeland—the diaspora is sometimes affirmed through another movement—engagement with the homeland. Movement, it could be argued, then, in its literal and metaphorical senses is at the heart the diasporic condition, beginning with the dispersal itself and culminating with reunification. The spaces in between are marked by multiple forms of engagement between the diaspora and the homeland—of movement, of travel between a "here" and a "there" both in terms of time and space.

Urban Intellectuals is the story of a young boy growing up at the knee of a man born during the Great Depression in the south who impressed upon the founder the importance of knowing thy history. As the boy comes of age, he notices the "miseducation" in the schools while gaining an appreciation for the power of the media, it's importance and how it can assist in educating and connecting the African Diaspora.

African diaspora aims to improve all articles related to the cultural contributions of people of African descent all over the world.

The term *African diaspora* gained currency from the 1950s and 1960s in the English-speaking world, especially the United States. As pointed out by George Shepperton, none of the major intellectual forerunners of African diaspora studies, from Edward Blyden (1832–1912), the influential nineteenth-century Caribbean-born Liberian thinker, to W. E. B. Du Bios (1868–1963), the renowned African-American scholar-activist, used the term African diaspora. The Negritude writers from Francophone Africa and the Caribbean also did not use it. Instead, the term used to define and mobilize African populations globally was Pan-Africanism. One of the challenges in African diaspora studies, then, has been to overcome an American and English language-centered model of identity for African diasporas globally.

Robert Franklin Williams' departure from his birthplace would classify him under the "African Diaspora" heading characterized within the model depicted as African diaspora English- speaking persons. For example, his ancestors were dispersed from Africa. Afterwards he was dispersed from the United States on phony kidnapping charges; and, therefore had to exile into Canada; and then Cuba for safety reasons. In Cuba a disagreement arose causing him to leave

Cuba for China where he lived for three years under Mao Zedong during the 1966 Beijing Cultural Revolution. Next from China his reunification back to the United States took place in 1996. A Multigenerational background: (UCensus Bureau defines multigenerational families as those consisting of more than two generations living under the same roof. Many researchers also include households with a grandparent and at least one other generation). Conscious of Africa as the homeland. Robert Franklin Williams: An intellectual rising from an upbringing with parents and grandparents who re-created, and restored the centrality of African diaspora in the making of the modern Black world-- grandmother was a former slave. His grandfather, a Republican, was the publisher of a local newspaper called The People's Voice; his ethos with *Legendary Pioneers of Black Radio;* the writing of *Negroes With Guns,* the writing publication and distribution of his *Crusader Magazine.*

In defining diaspora, there are several conceptual difficulties, especially in the case of African emphasis. The African diaspora—for example, indeed the term *diaspora causes* contemporary theorizations of the term *diaspora which* tend to be preoccupied with problematizing the relationship between diaspora and nation and the dualities or multiplicities of diasporic identity or subjectivity; they are inclined to be condemnatory or celebratory of transnational mobility and hybridity. In many cases, the term *diaspora* is used in a fuzzy, ahistorical, and uncritical manner in which all manner of movements and migrations between countries and even within countries are included and no adequate attention is paid to the historical conditions and experiences that produce diasporic communities and consciousness for instance how dispersed populations become self-conscious diaspora communities. The forced and brutal dispersal of millions of Africans into the foreign lands created the **African /Black Diaspora**. **African** slaves and their descendants carried skills and communitarian values, rich cultural traditions, resiliency, and resistance ethos: Robert Franklin Williams mode of behavior--defiance and self-reliance; ideas and civil rights deeds that transformed and enriched the cultures.

According to Tim Tyson, "The "African Diaspora" is generally understood to mean the people who have flowed out of Africa to all over the world; the whole of them imagined as one thing— the people of African descent, wherever they ended up and however they got there, what Marcus Garvey might have called the Black Nation. Yes, you are correct, your family, including Robert Franklin Williams, are clearly part of the African Diaspora, and would have been had they ended up in Brazil or Haiti or wherever. That would start considerably before Robert's grandmother's day, of course, though certainly she would come under the "African Diaspora" heading. 2020."

AFRICAN DIASPORA: Concepts, definitions, and History on **African diaspora** refers to the communities throughout the world that have resulted by descent from the movement in historic times of peoples from **Africa**, predominantly to the Americas and among other areas around the globe.

Negroes With Guns, Ann Coulter, refers to Robert F. Williams as a "Hero." She writes: "Liberals have leapt on the shooting death of Trayvon Martin in Florida to push for the repeal of "stand your ground" laws and to demand tighter gun control. (MSNBC'S Karen Finney blamed "the same people who stymied gun regulation at every point.")

*This would be like demanding more funding for the General Services Administration after seeing how its employees wasted taxpayer money on a party weekend in Las Vegas. *We don't know the facts yet, but let's assume the conclusion MSNBC is leaping to is accurate:

George Zimmerman stalked a small black child and murdered him in cold blood, just because he was black.

*If that were true, every black person in America should get a gun and join the National Rifle Association, America's oldest and most august civil rights organization.

Apparently, this has occurred to no one because it appears that our excellent public education system ensures that no American under the age of 60 has the slightest notion of this country's history.

*Gun control laws were originally promulgated by Democrats to keep guns out of the hands of blacks. This allowed the Democratic policy of slavery to proceed with fewer bumps and, after the Civil War, allowed the Democratic Ku Klux Klan to menace and murder black Americans with little resistance.

*(Contrary to what nonreaders believe, the KKK was an outgrowth of the Democratic Party, with overlapping membership rolls. The Klan was to the Democrats what the American Civil Liberties Union is today: Not every Democrat is an ACLUer, but every ACLUer is a Democrat. Same with the Klan.)

*In 1640, the very first gun control law ever enacted on these shores was passed in Virginia. It provided that blacks -- even freemen -- could not own guns.

*Chief Justice Roger Taney's infamous opinion in Dred Scott v. Sandford circularly argued that blacks could not be citizens because if they were citizens, they would have the right to own guns: "[I]t would give them the full liberty," he said, "to keep and carry arms wherever they went. *With logic like that, Republicans eventually had to fight a Civil War to get the Democrats to give up slavery. Alas, they were Democrats, so they cheated. After the war, Democratic legislatures enacted "Black Codes," denying black Americans the rights of citizenship -- such as the rather crucial one of bearing arms -- while other Democrats (sometimes the same Democrats) founded the Ku Klux Klan.

*For more than a hundred years, Republicans have aggressively supported arming blacks, so they could defend themselves against Democrats. The original draft of the Anti-Klan Act of 1871 -- passed at the urging of Republican president Ulysses S. Grant -- made it a federal felony to "deprive any citizen of the United States of any arms or weapons he may have in his house or possession for the defense of his person, family, or property." This section was deleted from the final bill only because it was deemed both beyond Congress' authority and superfluous, inasmuch as the rights of citizenship included the right to bear arms.

*Under authority of the Anti-Klan Act, President Grant deployed the U.S. military to destroy the Klan, and pretty nearly completed the job. But the Klan had a few resurgences in the early and mid-20th century. Curiously, wherever the Klan became a political force, gun control laws would suddenly appear on the books. This will give you an idea of how gun control laws worked. Following the firebombing of his house in 1956, Dr. Martin Luther King, who was, among other things, a Christian minister, applied for a gun permit, but the Alabama authorities found him unsuitable. A decade later, he won a Nobel Peace Prize.

Does that "may issue" gun permit policy work? The NRA opposed these discretionary gun permit laws and proceeded to grant NRA charters to blacks who sought to defend themselves from Klan violence—Including the great Robert Franklin Williams.

A World War II Marine veteran, Williams returned home to Monroe, N.C., to find the Klan riding high -- beating, lynching and murdering blacks at will. No one would join the NAACP for fear of Klan reprisals. Williams became president of the local chapter and increased membership from six to more than two-hundred.

But it was not until he obtained a charter from the NRA in 1957 and founded the Black Armed Guard that the Klan received their due "scare" in Monroe. Williams' repeated thwarting of violent Klan attacks is described in his stirring book, "Negroes With Guns." In one crucial battle, the Klan sieged the home of a black physician and his wife, but Williams and his Black Armed Guard stood sentry and repelled the larger, cowardly force. And that was the end of it.

As the Klan found out, it's not so much fun when the rabbit's got the gun.

The NRA's proud history of fighting the Klan has been airbrushed out of the record by those who were complicit with the KKK, Jim Crow and racial terror, to wit: the Democrats.

In the preface to *Negroes With Guns*, Williams writes: "I have asserted the right of Negroes to meet the violence of the Ku Klux Klan by armed self-defense -- and have acted on it. It has always been an accepted right of Americans, as the history of our Western states proves, that where the law is unable, or unwilling, to enforce order, the citizens can, and must act in self-defense against lawless violence. I believe this holds for black Americans as well as whites" (39). Contrary to MSNBC hosts, I do not believe the shooting in Florida is evidence of a resurgent KKK. But wherever the truth lies in that case, gun control is always a scheme of the powerful to deprive the powerless of the right to self-defense" (Coulter 2012).

****

But even the prophet of peace, the Reverend Doctor King was moved enough by Williams' logic to issue agreement of Williams' principles by stating that "when the Negro uses force in self-defense, he does not forfeit support- he may even win it, by the courage and self-respect it reflects."   Dr. Martin Luther King Jr.

Negroes with **Guns** is an account of how **Robert F. Williams** arrived at this belief in armed self-defense. To be clear, **Robert** never called for violent provocation by black individuals, "I do not mean that **Negroes** should go out and attempt to get revenge for mistreatments or injustices. I advocated for black individuals to defend themselves and the lives of their loved ones."

Robert F. Williams, leader of his local NAACP and one of the founders of the local NRA chapter. "An armed **person** is free, but a **disarmed person** is a subject. The War on Drugs succeeded in destroying the inner cities by breaking up families, and disenfranchising millions of minorities, and on the heels of this, modern day **gun** control has succeeded in leaving only criminals and violent gangs armed."

Photograph of Robert Franklin Williams. John Herman Williams' photos: University of Michigan, Bentley Library

"We as men should stand up as men and protect our women and children. I am a man, and I will walk upright as a man should. I will not crawl. I called for self-defense, not acts of war." Robert Franklin Williams words spoken at the 1959 NAACP convention.

Acknowledgments

A huge thank you is extended to all those who have supported this process: My loving family: beautiful children, grand-and great-grand-children, siblings, a host of nieces and nephews; cousins and their friends who have contributed by reading my works; tolerated me each time I began talking about my writing. They simply say, "We're so proud of you!" Bless their hearts.

The length of these acknowledgments reveals somewhat of my continued blessings. Thanks to my school colleagues, children, grand and great-grands, there are many. Dr. Timothy B. Tyson, Ph.D., at Duke University and Duke Divinity School for his benevolent willingness to answer questions. "Ask me anything; I will help wherever I can." He went on to add, "I am so glad to see that you're writing again," were his instant responses. The Wilkins and son Jeffrey L. Wilkins, Ph.D. North Carolina Central University for his diligent work in this project. Dr. Jeffrey Leak for the opportunity to present my first Robert F. Williams research at the conference on Lynching Without Sanctuary at UNC at Charlotte center city campus 2012. Dr. Janaka Lewis and Dr. Meg Morgan, UNCC colleagues. My church family members Reverend Doctor Leonzo D. Lynch and Nicole; Mercedes Thomas, Connie Brown, Margret Ross; Deacon Rick Hurt, Ivan M. Lowe. Antioch Baptist; Blessed Assurance; Mount Olive African Methodist;

and friends at Mount Carmel. And more recently, the ministers, congregation and business associates whom I met at the Church of God In Christ (COGIC) AIM Convention 2017 at the Charlotte, NC Convention Center, who prayed over my writing success; the Winchester Alumni Association; the Winchester Class Reunion of 62 they've presented and supported these works without hesitation. Robert & Lillie Heath; Lena Thompson; And especially to the Event Planning Team, Audrey Wallace, and Nadine Henry, of Affairs to Remember; Dot Siler and Ms. Gwyn at the McCrorey YMCA; Ms. C-Johnson at Hickory Grove Library and Sandy Seawright, who housed my first edition of *Emily's Blues* at Barnes and Noble in the late eighty's; he was also influential in introducing my titles to Ms. Vickie Chapman at West Boulevard Library; Maurice Trull at McEwen Funeral Service in Monroe—a lifetime family acquaintance; the illustrious Monroe Sherriff Mr. F. McGurit, Surluta Anthony of Monroe Local Government, The Williams and the Horton/Blackmon Family Reunions, Linda Colbert; Geneva Horton-Moore; Chester & Shirley Williams; D'Laval and Marlene Williams; Christopher and Cathy Williams; Carroll Williams; Shemeka and Corey McManus Senior Attorney McManus Law Firm; Gina Williams; Trudy & Vernard Wynn; the late Robin Sims and Makeda Davis; Rev. Mirthell & Rita Mitchell; Nephew, Patrick Williams; UNC, Charlotte Literary Festival; The Chessington Homeowners Association; Joe at Brothers Foreign Cars; Dr. Phillippi and Crystal; J. McDonald, Attorney at Law; High Top Construction; Fred at

Hendricks Motors; Folgers Car Dealership; Havertys Furniture; Ashley Furniture; Barbara Ann and nurses at Firsts Charlotte Physicians; Jennifer and Benjamin Winchester, CEO at **AllTech** Systems, Inc.; Jatrarious Laflare; Jerrytha Don and Keith; especially Madie-Gran-gran Taylor; Demetrice, Marina and Dawn Jordan; Pamela and Clint Stamps; Cleveland Huntly; Jacquelyn and Doris Williams; Joanett Moody; Sylvia Chisholm, Thurman Massey & The Massey family; Maria Macon, Myrtle and Pastor Moore; The Funderburkes; colleagues from the Big "G" high school: Viola Roseboro, Latarsha Roberts, Mariah King, Rachael Lloyd all says they can't wait to read it! Brenda Slade, the late Liz Williams, Jo Ella Ferrell; Jo Ann Smith, of course, Linda Hairston-always there with a smile, a chuckle, a willing spirit to edit; Bernice Smith; The McAuley's'(Ann); The Barretts, (Mary and Andrew); Maxine Hedgepeth; The Carlocks, Brian & Bobby; The Parrish family; Dr. Liesman, Pediatrist; Dr. "B" and all the "Bees" at Bilon Optometry; Johnson C. Smith University; Monroe Public Library; Leonard and Christine Glover, Shelia & Jerome Dickens; Dori Sanders Farm; the late Robin Brown and William Brown; Carol Johnson; Francine Black; Rosalind Crestfield; the late Wilma Owings, Walter Owings; Hazel Grier; Larry Crowder; Joan Mitchell all of whom have made a conscious effort to involve my works and or encourage this process whenever and wherever possible.

    For delaying the "putting some fresh eyes" on this work, any remaining imperfections in the book are entirely Robbie's fault—every single one of them! I thank you,

Robbie, my God-devoted mate who shares my religious beliefs and gives, over the many years, his steady support.

Book Review: Jeffrey L. Wilkins, PhD, Psychology Dept. North Carolina Central University

Audacity Story of A Legendary Hero by author Connie Williams is a biographical work that explores the life of civil rights activist Robert Franklin Williams (RFW). The book begins by setting up the historical and social context in which Robert F. Williams was born; 1920's Monroe, NC. RFW's life was wholly affected by the racial injustice, prejudice, and often violent environment that characterized life for Blacks in America.

Williams witnessed numerous incidents of hate and violence perpetrated by White Americans on those of African descent, including cross burnings, shootings and lynching by the KKK. These traumatic events shaped Williams into a local and national champion of racial equity. A defining characteristic of Williams's activism was a belief in armed self-reliance and self-defense. This belief ran counter to the prevailing ethos of the nonviolent protest espoused by the majority of civil rights leaders and organizations during that time.

Ms. Williams provides the reader with an array of seminal events that shaped RFW's ideology of self-defense. RFW increasingly became a local, then national figure in the civil rights movement of the mid to late 1950s and 60s. His repeated efforts to protect African Americans from race-based violence marked him as a primary target of reprisal from the KKK, local and federal law enforcement. As a result of these struggles, Williams became a leading figure in the civil rights movement in North Carolina and the US.

Themes, Ethos, Pathos, and Logos

Audacity provides the reader with a variety of themes; including race, prejudice, moral authority, and equality. *Ethos* represents the ethical appeal and the means by which the author convinces the audience of their credibility. Williams' account of the life of Robert Franklin Williams is well researched and entertaining to read. Williams has a deep understanding of the social, cultural, political and geographic context in which RFW lived. The author's expertise is drawn from her research into the writing of RFW and interviews with Robert Williams himself. Moreover, the author is a relative of RFW and was able to collaborated with the subject's family. This personal connection creates a sense of admiration and gratitude for the work of Robert Franklin Williams.

Pathos are the methods used by the author to appeal to the reader's emotions. Williams accomplishes this goal by providing episodic anecdotes of events throughout RFW's life. In particular, the author describes the traumatic and often violent encounters with white Americans RFW experienced. Williams' use of these events serves to draw the reader into the stark reality of the Jim Crow south and visualize the terror of lynching, shootings and cross burnings perpetrated by the KKK. Furthermore, the pathos of *Audacity* is one of admiration for the courage, integrity, and perseverance displayed by RFW.

Logos represents the use of logic and reason to appeal to the audience. Williams utilizes a historical, psychological, and cultural analysis to convince the audience that RFW is an all too often forgotten figure in the civil rights movement. The author argues that RFW's use of self-defense, radio, and writings should make him a more influential civil rights figure nationally, and not just in North Carolina. Williams employs Kohlberg's theory on moral development to suggest that RFW developed a post-conventional stage of moral reason. Furthermore, the author provides a developmental analysis of RFW based on theories of African American personality and Erikson's theory of psychosocial development. These analyses provide the reader with a deeper understanding of the psychological and identity crises RFW faced in his fight for racial, social, and legal equality for African Americans.

Williams includes a short excerpt from *Green*, a coming-of-age young adult novel about Emilee. Emilee is a child who comes of age in 1950's Morris town, a fictionalized representation of Monroe, NC. *Green* parallels the life of Robert Franklin Williams as written in *Audacity*. *Green* serves as an entertaining and instructive introduction to the struggles and violence African Americans faced throughout the southern United States in the 1950s-60s. *Green* would be most beneficial for middle grade and teenage youth, rather than younger children.

In conclusion, *Audacity Story of a Legendary Hero* is an entertaining and enlightening exposition of the life and contributions of Robert Franklin Williams to the civil rights movement. Connie Williams provides the reader with an authoritative, logical, and at times suspenseful examination of a legend of the civil rights movement. *Audacity* is an excellent addition to required reading lists for any class that seeks to critically examine historical, political, and social perspectives of race in America.

****

Chronology of Historical Even: Absent of Robert Franklin Williams, our legendary hero's accomplishment:1957 desegregation of the Monroe Library in NC:

1956 – United States presidential election, 1956 (Eisenhower re-elected)

- 1956 – "In God We Trust" adopted as national motto
- 1957 – Eisenhower Doctrine, wherein a country could request American economic assistance and/or aid from military forces if it was being threatened by armed aggression from another state
- 1957 – Civil Rights Act of 1957, primarily a voting rights bill, becomes the first civil rights legislation enacted by Congress since Reconstruction
- 1957 – Soviets launch Sputnik; "space race" begins
- 1957 – Shipping port Atomic Power Station, the first commercial nuclear power plant in the U.S., goes into service
- 1957 – Little Rock, Arkansas school desegregation
- 1958 – National Defense Education Act
- 1958 – NASA formed as the U.S. begins ramping up efforts to explore space
- 1959 – The NBC western *Bonanza* becomes the first drama to be broadcast in color
- 1959 – Cuban Revolution
- 1959 – Landrum–Griffin Act, a labor law that regulates labor unions' internal affairs and their officials' relationships with employers, becomes law
- 1959 – Alaska and Hawaii became the 49th and 50th U.S. states; to date, they are the final two states admitted to the union.

1960s in the United States: 1960, 1961, 1962, 1963, 1964, 1965, 1966, 1967, 1968, 1969.

- 1960 – U-2 incident, wherein a CIA U-2 spy plane was shot down while flying a reconnaissance mission over Soviet Union airspace
- 1960 – Greensboro sit-ins, sparked by four African American college students refusing to move from a segregated lunch counter, spurs similar actions and increases sentiment in the Civil Rights Movement.
- 1960 – Civil Rights Act of 1960, establishing federal inspection of local voter registration polls and penalties for those attempting to obstruct someone's attempt to register to vote or actually vote
- 1960 – National Front for the Liberation of Vietnam formed
- 1960 – United States presidential election, 1960 (John F. Kennedy elected president)
- 1961 – US breaks diplomatic relations with Cuba
- 1961 – Eisenhower gives celebrated "military–industrial complex" farewell address
- 1961 – John F. Kennedy becomes President
- 1961 – 23rd Amendment, which grants electors to the District of Columbia
- 1961 – Peace Corps established.
- 1961 – Alliance for Progress
- 1961 – Bay of Pigs Invasion
- 1961 – Alan Shepard pilots the Freedom 7 capsule to become the first American in space
- 1961 – Trade embargo on Cuba

- Historical Events of Robert Franklin Williams should be added

- 1957 – Robert Franklin Williams becomes president of the NAACP.
- 1957 – Desegregated Monroe's Union County Library
- 1960 – Robert Franklin Williams becomes an international presence in the "Famous Monroe Kissing" Incident

- 1961 - Robert F. Williams leads a group of Black children who
- attempted to integrate the tax supported pool in Monroe, NC.
- 1961 - Robert F. Williams & Armed Self-Defense in Monroe, NC
- 1961 – Frame-up Escape & Exile of Robert Franklin Williams
- 1962 - Robert Franklin Williams in Cuba and Radio Havana Cuba wrote Negroes With Guns
- 1965 - RFW in China
- 1969 – 1975 RFW return to US prearrangement of President Richard Nixon.
- 1975 – RFW tried in Monroe, NC court: All Charges dropped
- 1975 – Published a militant journal "Crusader"
- 1975 – Ford Foundation grant /University of Michigan Center for Chinese Studies. Wrote *While God Lay Sleeping*: The Autobiography of Robert F. Williams.

Notes

African Diaspora. (Defining). January 13, 2018

American Labor Party (ALP) In 1936 was formed by left-wing supporters of Franklin D. Roosevelt and the New Deal. was formed by left-wing supporters of Franklin D. Roosevelt and the New Deal. 30

Barger, Robert N. A SUMMARY OF LAWRENCE KOHLBERG'S STAGES OF MORAL DEVELOPMENT Copyright 2000 by Robert N. Barger, Ph.D. University of Notre Dame Notre Dame, IN 46556

Black Scholar, The: Covering a wide variety of subject areas and incorporating the journal imprints of Routledge, Carfax, Spon Press, Psychology Press, Martin Dunitz, and Taylor & Francis.

Bronfenbrenner, vi. Ecological Systems Theory. Vygotsky's Sociocultural Theory deo: o47 (1960). (this theory was key in changing the perspective of developmental psychology by calling attention to a large number of environment social influences on a child's development.

Borkar).By Rujuta Borkar Published: 2-18-2011: 69

Category: African-American Related
   Posted: February 27, 2010

Catterall, B. "It all came together." Cornel West from his lecture/rap given at Berkeley. 2002.

City Council, Monroe, NC 1958.3-21-26. Negroes and the Gun: The Black Tradition of Arms by ...https://www.barnesandnoble.com/w/negroes-and-the...The city council agreed. In an emergency meeting, it passed an ordinance banning KKK motorcades. On October 5, 1957, when the Klan motorcade, led by Cole and police chief Mauney fired into Dr. Perry's house, members of the Monroe Rifle Club fired back from behind breastworks they had constructed. They fired low and did not hit anyone in the motorcade. The Klan members ran off, and the Monroe City Council banned Klan motorcades the next day.

Clark, F. Professor F. Clark Power of the University of Notre Dame (a former student of Kohlberg's) and to Professor Steve Chilton of the University of Minnesota for suggestions concerning this summary: 64.

****

Interview with Brother D'Lavel: "Secrets Drug Store in the 60s, it was necessary for Blacks to go through the store to arrive where we could be served. Some of the favorite places were Oasis; 5 Points; Blue Bird Grill; Royal Gardens right next door to Ace Crowell, the undertaker's Mortuary. Stores were Winford Helms; VB Baucom's store on Winchester Avenue. A Historical and remembered moment: Big Six slapped Bro. Byrd down, but he got right back up again and walked away as if nothing had happened. Big Six unfortunately loss her life one night at the American Legion Club after being shot six times allegedly by her boyfriend."

Interview with Sister Pat: "Daddy said, get down on the floor." I asked, "What were you doing?" She said, "We were looking out of the window, but Daddy didn't know it. We were trying to see the motorcade of the KKK coming down our street, Fairley Avenue." I asked, "What were you thinking?" "If any one of those MF set foot on this porch, I hope Daddy will shoot the s--- out of him." I asked, "What were your school mates talking about?" "At Winchester, Avenue School we went on about what we were supposed to do. Everything was segregated. *Them* "Crackers" didn't want an up-rising in the school because they didn't want integration."

Price, Jimmy. /The Columbia Record/AP. The true story of George Stinney Jr. and his brutal execution. 140.

Ruodi, Duan et al. "Our Forty-Four Years of Struggle Must End Now." 2016. 126

PRJ Think: Communiversity: Interview with Honorable Robert F. Williams. Message 2D a Grassroots Where Learning is a Life Long Progress (April 2014). 120

Race Riot of 1943: Detroit Historical Society. 24

Robert Williams in China: From a Promoter for Armed Revolution to a Nonviolence Activist, 1963–69 the question of the legitimate use of violence. consider what can be meant by the "global 1960s." It will also stage discussions on key ideas about the sixties, such as Black Power and Third World issues, that transformed understandings of race, ethnicity, and power. 125

Ruodi Duan is a Ph.D. candidate in Harvard's History Department researching race and ethnic studies in the Cold War, with a focus on Chinese depictions of African American social movements. **"Our Forty-Four Years of Struggle Must End Now." 2016.** 126

This article received an "honorable mention" in the Fairbank Centers 2016 Travel Essay Competition. 126

(See more from): Republic of China in the United Nations (1945–1971). From Wikipedia, the free encyclopedia https://en.wikipedia.org/wiki/Enver_Hoxh a. 135

Tyson, Timothy B. A quote: U.S. Senator J. Helms used with permission. Email from T. Tyson to author. July 2, 2019. 92

Tyson, Timothy B. "Defining African Diaspora." Email response from T. Tyson to author, Connie Williams. August 13, (2020). 152-153

Undesirable Discharge: Law and Legal Definition Undesirable discharge refers to an administrative discharge under "conditions other than honorable." It is generally given to a member of the military who does not qualify for an honorable discharge. An undesirable discharge does not involve punishment. US definitions.uslegal.com/u/undesirable-discharge/ Experience: Retired **Marine** Corps lawyer and Veterans Services Officer (VSO) with 12+ yrs. of experience. Verified. Thanks for the chance to assist Currently there is no longer an **"undesirable"** discharge…

https://www.theblaze.com/news/2012/10/01/allen.

"We don't intend to be lynched" words of Robert Williams. 32-40

Williams, Connie. "Military Guns and Ammunition." Interview with Jones McConnie Williams a WWII Veteran, 1 Aug. 1989. 48.

Williams, Connie. "Our black heroes killed..." Interview with Robert F. Williams. 1985: 112.

Williams, Connie. "My Life." Interview with Robert F. Williams. 3 July. 1989.

Williams, Connie: Googleapps.com UNC, Charlotte, Web site. Multimodal Project. Negroes with Guns
 (video 217) Robert F. Williams

Williams, Connie. Personal interview: Family Reunion. Holiday Inn with R.F. Williams. 2 July, 1984 144-145.

Williams, Mabel, wife of RFW, "the interracial liberalism in Union County collapsed because of the deeply racial prejudices, there seemed to be a backlash against Ray Shute and other white liberals who backed off when blacks prepared to fight back" (Monroe Enquirer 1957).

Williams, Marvin. "The Robert F. Williams' family members." Conference call to author, Connie Williams, August 20, 2020.

Williams Research Papers. 111

Williams, Reverend John Chalmer. Telephone conference with author. "Research, Anti-lynching, Story of a Hero" looks good." 16 Sept. 2012.

Williams, Robert Franklin Photos in this publication, *Audacity: Story of a Hero*, Connie Williams, obtained via Family Reunions; media, press, newspaper releases; John H.

Williams archives   University of Michigan, Bentley Library. 129, 130, 131, 132,   136, 159.

Williams Papers, 1959 *Negroes with Guns* (Africanization 101) Kujichagulia Productions and TCA Media.

Williams, Robert F. of Monroe, in Union County, contributed to a controversy over violence and nonviolence within the Civil Rights movement in the late 1950s. 134.

Williams, Robert Franklin. "Famous Monroe Kissing Incident of 1960." 50-54.

Worley et al 1987 "King and Williams on Non Violence" 102.

Selected Bibliography

A Forgotten Hero Of Black History: Robert F. Williams, A Negro With A Gun 27. Feb: 2010

Arsenault, Raymond. Freedom Rider: 1961 and the Struggle for Racial Justice. Oxford University Press: 2006. 43-44.

August, Meier, Elliot Rudwick, and Francis L. Broderick, Bobbs-Merrill, el edited:1971. *Document: Robert F 1925 modified 3-9- 2015: D Black Protest Thought in the Twentieth Century.*

Blair, Clay Jr. *The Strange Case of James Earl Ray The Man Who Murdered Martin Luther King.* New York: A Bantam Book, 1967-1969.

Borkar).By Rujuta Borkar Published: 2-18-2011

Burns, Jack, article: Apr 15, 2018 · **Robert F. Williams** and the 'Black 16.

Catterall, B. "It all came together." Cornel West from his lecture/rap given at Berkeley. 2002.

Chesnutt: In the Classroom: faculty.berea.edu/ Browners/ Chesnutt/classroom/lynching. 6.

Clark, F. Professor F. Clark Power of the University of Notre Dame (a former student of Kohlberg's) and to Professor Steve Chilton of the University of Minnesota for suggestions concerning this summary: 64.

Cohen, Robert Carl, *Black Crusader: A Biography of Robert Franklin Williams*, Stuart, 1972. 27-30.

Complexity of the U.S.-China relations in the 1960s. Hongshan Li, Kent State University, January 6, 2018

Crain, Williams, C., "Kohlberg's Stages of Moral Development" Theories of Development, concepts and application. Prentice-Hall, Inc. Englewood, New Jersey 1985 118-136

Cross et al 1990. 13

Daniels: Charlotte Observer Newspaper. 22

Davis, Perry, Harris. China A History of the World. Houghton Mifflin: 1985

Drimmer, Melvin. "Lynching." **Black History**. New York: Anchor Books Doubleday & Company, Inc., 1968.

Duan, Ruodi, Ph.D. Harvard's History Department. "Race and ethnic studies in the Cold War, with a focus on Chinese depictions of African American social movements." "honorable mention" in the Fairbank Centers 2016.

Elliston, John. Psywar on Cuba: "The Declassified History of US Anti-Castro Propaganda." Ocean Press. July, 2002 81 en.wikipedia.org/wiki/Wikipedia: AFRO - Cached

Erikson, Erik's Stages of Development. 107-109.

Foner, Phillip S., *The Black Panthers Speak*, Da Capo, 1995.

Forman, James, *The Making of Black Revolutionaries*, Open Hand, 1972. 46-47.

Geschwender, James A., *The Black Revolt: The Civil Rights Movement, Ghetto Uprisings, and Separatism*, Prentice Hall, 1971.

Greve, E. (2012, March, 10) Republic of New Africa (1968). Retrieved from https://www.blackpast.org/african-ameican-history/republic-newafrica-1968/

Haley, Alex. **The Autobiography of Malcolm X.** New York: Grove Press, Inc. 1965.

Harris et al 2007. 13

Havighurst's Developmental Tasks Theory (Harris 138).

Hongshan Li. Complexity of the U.S.-China relations in the 1960s. Kent State University, January 6, 2018

Hughes, Langston, "Nuff Said." Panther and the Lash, John Cohassey.

James, Beverly; Stephanie Banchero. News stories on Robert F. Williams. The Charlotte Observer 26 Feb; 19 Mar. 1995.

Kambon, Kobi K.K. and Terra Bowen-Reid. Department of Psychology. Florida A & M University. 2012.

Kohlberg, Lawrence, *Collected Papers on Moral Development and Moral_ Education*, Spring 1973.

Kohlberg, Lawrence, The Psychology of Moral Development, Essays on Moral   Development, Harper and Row Publishers, San Francisco, 1984.

Kohlberg, Lawrence and Others, "Reading in Moral Education," Library of Congress, Catalog and card Number 77-82606, Winston Press Inc., 1978. 92

Lokos, Lionel, *The New Racism: Reverse Discrimination in America*, Arlington House, 1971.

Lynch mob mentality. English dictionary 2010. 44.

Malcolm X. "To Mississippi Youth." Worley, Demetrice A. et al. **African American Literature**. Illinois:

National Textbook Company, 1987. Monroe Enquirer 1957. 121.

Negroes with Guns (ReAfrikanization 101) Kujichagulia Productions and TCA Media

Neumann, Eric. Depth Psychology and a New Ethic, "Scapegoat Psychology" trans. Eugene Rolfe (Putnam; N.Y. : 1969): 49-58.

No Guns for Negros: (Part I : 20:39). (A slave is a person who is disarmed). Oliver 1989; Ward 1995

Parham and Helms. Black Racial Identity: Oliver 1989; Ward   1995. 97-98.

Powell, William S. *Encyclopedia of North Carolina.* 2006: the University of North Carolina Press.

Parks, Rosa and Connie Williams, North Carolina. Personal photographs by author. 22 October 1996. 160.

Piaget's Theory of Cognitive Development

Price, Jimmy. /The Columbia Record/AP

Power, Clark F. .Professor of the University of Notre Dame (a former student of Kohlberg's) and to Professor Steve Chilton of the University of Minnesota for suggestions concerning this summary.

Shapiro, Herbert, *White Violence and Black Response*, University of Massachusetts, 1988. Rest 1979 8.

The NC Museum of History: Robert F. Williams

The Single Issue in the Robert Williams Case, **NAACP** townhall.com/columnists/Ann coulter/2012/04/18/negroes-with-guns- n1179191.

Self-Defense in the Civil Rights Movement: the Lessons of Birmingham, 1963 MICHAEL BARKER
DECEMBER 10, 2019

Shapiro, Herbert, *White Violence and Black Response*, University of Massachusetts, 1988: 46.

Swales, John. "Gene Analysis: English in Academic and Research Settings." *Writing*

About Writing. New York: Bedford/St. Martin's, 2011. 19.

Tyson, Timothy B. Radio Free Dixie: Robert F. Williams & the Roots of Black Power. North Carolina: The University of North Carolina Press. 1999: 21, 42-43.

vi Bronfenbrenner's Ecological Systems Theory

Vygotsky's Sociocultural Theory deo: 047 (1960).

Wiki Project: African diaspora

Williams, John Chalmer. "Re. Story of a Hero, Robert F. Williams." Email to the author. 1 July, 2012.

Williams, Marvin. "The Robert F. Williams' family members." Conference call to author, Connie Williams, August 20, 2020.

Williams Papers, 1959 *Negroes with Guns* (ReAfrikanization 101) Kujichagulia Productions and TCA Media.

Williams, Robert Franklin. "Famous Monroe Kissing Incident of 1960."

Williams, Robert Franklin. No Guns for Negros: (Part I : 20:39). ("A slave is a person who is disarmed").

Williams, Robert Franklin, Negro With Guns, "An NAACP Chapter is Reborn in Militancy" (50). Martino Publishing. CT: 2013: 32-39

Williams, Robert F. "Prologue." *Negroes With Guns.* 2013: 39. Martino Publication, Mansfield Centre, CT. 32-39.

Williams, Robert F., *Negroes With Guns*, Marzani & Munsell, 1962 (reprinted by Third World Press, 1973).

Williams, Robert. Swimming Pool Showdown, *Southern Exposure.* John Cohassey

Williams, Connie. "A Hero-- Lineage" excerpt: **This Life: Through Grace Hope Mercy.** North Carolina: A Williams Acorn Press, 2019: p257-258.

Williams, Robert F. **Negroes With Guns.** Chicago: Third World Press, 1972.

Williams, Connie. Personal interview with R.F. Williams. 2 July, 1985.

Williams, Robert F. *Negros With Guns.* 2013: Martino Publishing

Worley et al 1987 "King and Williams on Non Violence

Internet

Erikson Stages of Psychosocial Development in Plain Language. 107.

https://www.healthline.com/health/parenting/erikson-stages. 104.

en.wikipedia.org/wiki/Robert_F._Williams. 15.

https://blackamericaweb.com/2016/04/01/little-known-black-history-fact-robert-f-williams

https://www.blackpast.org/african-american-history/republic-new- africa-1968. 125.

https://caribbean.commons.gc.cuny.edu/2019/04/09/black-intellectuals-and-the-making-of...

https://camron46.blogspot.com/2014/11/robert-f-williams-important-african.html. 135.

https://timeline.com/klan-family-values-539be2ff7f55. 54.

http://pages.uncc.edu/newsouth2012conference/news/. 7.

https://plato.stanford.edu/entries/civil- disobedience

https://www.coursehero.com/file/pj1g5qq/Rest-1979...

https://**detroit**historical.org/learn/**encyclopedia-of-detroit/race-riot-** 1943. 26.

https://en.wikipedia.org/Wiki/National_Rifle_Associati on. 45.

*https://**en.wikipedia.org**/wiki/**Enver_Hoxha**

https://face2faceafrica.com/support/ **The Truth About Muhammad Ali and The Draft | Ali Draft Evasion**

https://jorvikpress.com/books/black-crusade

https://www.kent.edu/history/profile/hongshan-li. 126.

https://www.oldest.org./people/human-skeletons/. 155.

https://www.urbandictionary.com/define.php?term=Leftist

https://newsone.com/playlist/black-men-boy-who-were-killed-by-police

https://**quizlet.com**/32430214/**black-social-movements-in-the-us-**

https://www.coursehero.com/file/pj1g5qq/Rest-1979...

https://www.theblaze.com/news/2012/10/01/allen...

https://rbgstreetscholar.wordpress.com/2014/04/25

https://ufdc.ufl.edu/AA00032819/00001. Helms "Internalization" 146 TAAC. (Parham & Helms...)

https://archive.org/details/whiteviolencebla0000shap 46

https://en.wikipedia.org/wiki/Fusion_Party pp 20.

https://urban**intellectuals**.com/about

https://www.salon.com/2010/02/05/Lynch_mobs

https://**www.wcnc.com**/video/**news**/local/legacy-of-**lynching-**exhibit- to-open-**at-levine (2019).**

https://www.encyclopedia.com/.../robert-franklin-williams (Newton, Huey P.117).

King, Martin Luther Jr. :https://www.ncronline.org/.../**what-martin- luther-king-jr-can-teach-us-about-nonviolence.**

www.brookings.edu/blog/how-we-rise/2020/07/23/five-things-john-lewis-taught-u. 156

About the Author

Photo curtesy of Hawaii: 2019

Connie Williams is a local figure known for her distinguished career as a skillful writer of prose and poetry. Until her retirement in 2014 she was an instructor of English Composition and Rhetoric at UNC, at Charlotte; a high school English instructor at Charlotte-Mecklenburg Schools and Union

County Schools. Her first book, an inspirational, fictionalized autobiography, **Emily's Blues,** tells how a young divorcee and mother of four, went from poverty to a professional and was showcased in the "Dare to Dream Project", Z Smith Reynolds Foundation, 1990. She is the recipient of the Arts and Science Council Emerging Artist Award for *Emily's Blues.* Her novel's stage play adaptation, entitled "Emily's Dilemma," received the Honorable Terry Sanford Award for Creativity Honorable Mention, and was performed at Livingstone College at Salisbury by her students.

Her dedication to arts education and outreach led Williams to create, the Emily's Blues Self-Actualization Project, and she volunteered her services to help deter high school dropouts. The program received the Union County Community Arts Council Award for eight years at Piedmont High School where her book was used with students. She has volunteered her services to Healthy Mothers and Healthy Babies, the University of South Carolina, at Lancaster; International Young Writers Program, in Charlotte. She has presented readings and facilitated writing workshops at: Barnes and Noble, the Charlotte Public Library, Imagine On, Ebenezer Baptist Church, the Nile Theater, and UNC, Center City Campus at Charlotte; Spirit Square, Charlotte; Afro American Cultural Center, Charlotte. She is a Christa McAuliffe Fellow finalist.

She is a contributing author to the following publications: "Mama Allie's Talking Dogs..."

stories and recipes of Carolina cuisine, **Hungry for Home,** Rogers. Novello Festival Press: 2003. A short story excerpt, **Emily's Blues**, and a collection of poetry, **The National Literary Circular**: 1990. Original poetry, **A Sun-filled Dream**: 1989. She is the recipient of The National Library of Poetry, Editor's Choice Award for outstanding achievement in Poetry, 1998, for her poem entitled "Hands," dedicated to her father, Jones McConnie Williams, WWII Army veteran. Classroom consultant: **A History of the World** textbook: Houghton Mifflin: Boston. 1988. Williams is the recipient of the 1996 North Carolina Arts Council Award and The National Endowment for the Arts Award for a Fellowship at Headlands Center for the Arts, Sausalito, California, as an eight weeks artist heir. She is a former Writing Fellow of the University of North Carolina, at Charlotte, 1992. A native of Monroe, North Carolina, she has eleven siblings. Her parents Jones and Lillie Williams celebrated their 68th wedding anniversary 2009 and passed shortly afterward in 2010 and 2011 within four months apart.

In 2015 Williams started her own publication company an AWAP imprint, (A Williams' Acorn Publication) and published her first novel GREEN, 2015 under her imprint. She published a second edition of *EMILY'S BLUES in 2016*; additionally, a third novel entitled *JON AND LALE'S DANCE in 2018*; and in 2019 a fifth book—an inspirational testimony entitled, *THIS LIFE: THROUGH GRACE HOPE MERCY*.

Williams is a wife, proud mother of four daughters; three of the children are at rest with our Lord. She is also a grand and great- grandmother. She graduated from Cal State University, Northridge (B.A. Degree), and the University of North Carolina, at Charlotte (M.Ed. Degree). She resides with her husband in North Carolina.

Commentary about writing *Audacity* by the author: A rich process of discovery that might have both private and public value. Academic and professional writers develop a sense of rhetorical purpose as the process unfolds, not strictly before the act of researching and writing.

So, writers/researchers need to collect data and write with an established and focused sense of their goal (deliberate work), but it is necessary to adapt and consider unforeseen data and insights that are discovered during the process (method of effort), warrants further examination.
Although Piaget and Kohlberg's theory on moral development is well referenced-- laid the foundation for study, I must note the importance that culture, social class and especially family values played in the moral development of Robert Franklin Williams.
The hypothesized scenario used in Kohlberg's research inadequately represent the moral situation Robert Franklin Williams's encountered in an unexpected daily experience that prompted moral dilemmas per se.
I contend that family practices provided for RFW opportunities to systematically teach structure of moral reasoning. For Example, advances in moral development generated from RFW's own thinking about moral problems. It is surprising that Kohlberg's view on the importance that the

role of the family plays in the development of moral reasoning. Carol Gilligan (1982) contends that caring for both self and others (Postconventional Level) care becomes a universal duty to the individual and others. RFW demonstrated this care for others first as a young boy, to be precise, the development and use of the X35 preventing harm against vulnerable and unprotected females of color during the 50s and 60s which set this pattern of protection for his life. Additionally, we see it when [the Montgomery event; the Kissing Case; protection for Dr. Perry's home; the call for Black men to stand up and protect their families, their property and themselves].

Although Kohlberg's stages 5 and 6 are rarely ever achieved, however, according to Carol Gilligan (1982) Theory of Ethnic Care, emphasized that "the most advanced moral reasoning stage (Systemic and Standard) occurs when one's moral base is centered on the maintenance of basic human rights and values for others in their social system.
Robert Franklin Williams actions in the situation with the swimming pool experience, is another case in point of universal duty, when a young black boy lost his life while swimming in a local mud hole, when Mr. Williams makes the conscious decision to move to action to prevent further life threatening occurrences, he moved to integrate the tax dollars supported integrated Monroe Country Club swimming pool so that black children would benefit

from the safety provided there, the same as their white counterparts.

Of course, as in any research, this issue warrants further examination.

The limitations of Kohlberg's scenarios argues that moral development should be measured using multiple methods (a series of hypothetical moral dilemmas). That the Kohlberg research do not adequately represent the moral situations that many children and adolescents encounter in everyday experiences.

But in the analysis of the everyday encounters Robert Franklin Williams endured growing up under lynch laws in Monroe, North Carolina, the cultural climate of blacks' vs whites certainly influenced his moral judgement also of equal importance are community equity and collective happiness that must be considered.

Further repercussions followed the swimming pool demonstrations event when The KKK head dragon, James's "Catfish" Cole led a revival in nearby Salisbury. He later told a crowd of two thousand whites, "a '*nigger*' who wants to go to a white swimming pool is not looking for a bath, he is LOOKNG FOR A FUNERAL."—I term this statement as a clear case of *lynch-mob mentality*. It's just pure mob mentality: an authority figure appears and affixes a demonizing other label to someone's forehead, and the adoring crowd – "frothing- at -the -mouth" and feeding on each other's hatred (English dictionary 2010).

****

In the words of Raymond Arsenault, "In fact, in the same year that the SCLC was founded, the former head of the Monroe, North Carolina, chapter of the NAACP, Robert Williams — a one-time soldier who was not so enamored by the emancipatory potential of pacificism – formally created a locally-based self-defense organization to repel Klan violence in his neighborhood. However, *what made the gun-toting Williams's most controversial, was not his commitment to self-defense per se, but it was his vocal advocacy for "armed self-reliance" within the violently segregated towns of the South. Unsurprisingly it was his active and very vocal opposition to the pacifist doctrine of the mainstream civil rights leaders that contributed to his notoriety.* Highlights in his insightful history of this period *Freedom Riders…*: "Nowhere in the annals of history does the record show a people delivered from bondage by patience alone" (2006).

Malcolm X once said about Williams, "He was a man a little before his time." Beyond this, Williams and Malcolm X were supporters of the same cause; they often communicated via telephone on matters of civil rights. Malcolm's ideas were derived through Williams's original foundation. Robert Williams was a forerunner in ideas of armed, self-reliance. But Williams's name isn't included in most present-day accounts of the civil rights movement. He is little remembered even in his home state, where his argument that blacks should arm themselves against the threat of violence by segregationist whites earned him at the height of his notoriety, (and I, as the author of this biography, would also note, it earned him the most unfortunate and disrespectful label) a "violent crusader."

Other works by Connie Williams

Emily Blues
A fictionalized autobiography based on a true story by Connie Williams

1989, Connie Williams gained recognition for her first book, entitled **Emily's Blues**, a fictionalized autobiography, an excellent portrayal of a young girl in the 60s as she searched relentlessly for identity and a better life in an oppressive society. Her struggle to find dignity and self-worth should inspire girls around the globe to fight for the freedom and the respect they deserve. All females will find something relative to their lives in this emotional saga as Emily journeys from North Carolina, to New York, New Jersey, Washington, DC, and finally she makes an East to West odyssey in California to overcome. The story should serve as a wake-up call to males who are abusive to females or refuse to acknowledge their worth and importance. It should encourage fathers to become more involved in preparing their daughters for the pitfalls they might encounter in their relationships with males. **L. Hairston, Charlotte-Mecklenburg Schools**

While a teacher in the Union County School System, Williams founded The Emily's Blues Self-Actualization Project, a program designed to help deter school dropouts. Williams later penned "Emily's Dilemma," a stage play adaptation from her book that was performed at Livingstone College by her students, and received Honorable Mention by the Honorable Terry Sanford for an Arts Education Projects, supported by the Union County Community Arts Council in 1990. Emily's Blues was republished again in 2016. As a writer and educator, Williams wrote Emily's Blues to show young readers how she became "unstoppable" in overcoming an oppressed and impoverished background to get an education and become a professional educator. She received the Arts and Science Council Emerging Artist Award for Emily's Blues.

Emily's Blues is available at stores, online at Amazon and on Amazon Kindle

Green, a novel based on a true story by Connie Williams

    1996, while a Writing Fellow at Headlands Center for the Arts, Sausalito, California, through an Award from the North Carolina Arts Council and the National Endowment for the Arts, Williams began writing her second book, **Green**, a historical novel set in Monroe, North Carolina during the civil rights upheaval of the late 50s. Complicated, insightful, instructive and moving--with devastating guilt over the cause of a cornerstone family member's death-a precocious, eleven year old tri-racial girl, comes of age in Morris Town, a small city in North Carolina in the early 1960s. Emilee shows us her sensitive and very personal perception as she witnesses and learns of history via the refined extended family members during the South's Civil Rights Movement led by her cousin, the NAACP President, Robert F. Williams-"RW"--in Morris

Town, North Carolina. As Emilee tries to understand her layered world of death, difficult relationships and her own identity, her world heaves with rebel flag waving Ku Klux Klansmen's deliberate racial violent upheaval as their motorcades ride right pass her window on Fairley Avenue.

Frye Gaillard, author and winner of the Alabama Library Association Book of the Year Award says, "Good description, good imagery and deliberate repetition. **GREEN** is an intriguing story."

The late, **Minister John C. Williams, son of Robert F. Williams quotes,** "I believe the work will do great things for young audiences who otherwise would know nothing about the late Robert F. Williams, the Civil Rights Activists. The history is relevant and important today."

Available at stores: Barnes and Noble online, Amazon, Books-a-Million and in six different countries!

Jon and Lale's Dance, a novel based on a true story by Connie Williams

Williams' third novel, *Jon and Lale's Dance* is the story that she was compelled to write. It is the narrative of her parents who were married for 68 years before their passing in 2010 and 2011 within four months of each other around the time of their birthdays.

Sixty plus years of marriage have gone by, and the couple, Jon and Lale, find themselves still totally devoted to each other, yet they cannot resist the daily temptations, from time to time, to slip back into their old habits of agitating each other at the most inopportune moments. Lale can't manage to leave the house to grocery shop for necessities with her daughter, Topia, for Jon's Doctor Pepper and jar of his favorite Jiffy peanut butter, without first "directing some insults" toward him about his need to "sit, do nothing and nap" at the kitchen table. And Jon cannot manage to resist using his quick-wit of accusations that stops Lale in her tracks each time she makes an attempt to prepare to leave the house, to get into the car with her daughter, Topia. And this is how their battles usually begin, that sometimes last all afternoon, until Jon wants to nap again. They each enjoy satirizing. Williams threads this story with humor, suspense, tragedy and the true-to-life sensitive facts about health issues such as dementia, crippling rheumatoid arthritis and cancer that so many families and senior citizens face, that may lead to their sometimes early demise in today's society.

Available at Amazon, Barnes and Noble, Books-a-Million and other vendors including foreign markets.

Confession of the Onion Ring King: A children's story for all ages, 2019.

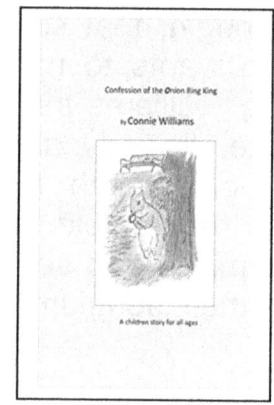

    This is Williams' first published children story and her fourth book. This story tells about a mischievous squirrel that gets into trouble in the human world.

All available at bookstores and online at Amazon.

This Life: Through Grace Hope Mercy, an inspirational testimony, is Williams's fifth book.

Growing up with her parents and ten siblings in North Carolina, Williams had a close relationship with her Lord and Savior. In *This Life: Through Grace, Hope and Mercy*, Williams shares her inspirational testimony of God's favor. In the nineteen chapter narrative, Williams leaves nothing to ambiguity; she holds nothing back, as her readers experience the riveting beginning episode in the San Fernando Valley where she evades what could have been premeditated murder of a friend, to the core shaken falling action—escaping death numerous times, when saved in North Carolina, New Jersey, New York, Washington, DC, Compton and Hollywood by nothing short of divine intervention-- miracles of the Lord's salvation.

Williams comes to understands that God's favor is to show His purpose for her life which she so often reveals throughout the work in words of scripture: "And **call upon me** in **the** day of trouble; I will deliver you, and you shall **glorify** me" (Psalm 50:15).

Coming soon: Other works by Connie Williams.

©*Snappy Feet, Miss Beasley and Bushy Tail, (A children's story)*.
©*Miss Beasley Runs Away, (A children's story)*.
©*Discovering Daddy*, a novel.
©*Short Stories the Breads of Life* (a cookbook including short stories).
©*Remembered*, a book of poetry.
© *Qak-Qak, What are We Supposed to Do*, a novel?
©*Untied Shoelaces*, a novel.
©*Forward Move Backwards*, a novel.
©*Mysterious Mac (unauthorized biography)*.
©*Oxymoronic*, a controversial book.
©*What Drives Miss Dorie*, (an authorized biography).
©*When the Tires Stopped Rolling*, a novel.
©*The Head Start Program*, Educational research prose.

Blank

Blank

00035
25.⁰⁰

Made in the USA
Middletown, DE
29 December 2022

18113527R10136